Walking with Jesus

...Reflections of those who knew Him

Father Daniel Sullivan

Paulist Press
New York/Mahwah, N.J.

Scripture extracts are taken from the New Revised Standard Version, Copyright © 1989, by the Division of Christian Education of the National Council of the Churches of Christ in the United States of America and reprinted by permission of the publisher.

Cover & interior design by Lynn Else

Library of Congress Cataloging-in-Publication Data

Sullivan, Daniel, 1949–
    Walking with Jesus : reflections of those who knew him / by
Daniel Sullivan.
        p. cm.
    ISBN 0-8091-4131-0
    1. Jesus Christ—Biography—Meditations. 2. Jesus Christ—Friends
and associates. I. Title.
    BT306.43 .S85 2002
    232.9′01—dc21

                                                    2002153722

Published by Paulist Press
997 Macarthur Boulevard
Mahwah, New Jersey 07430

www.paulistpress.com

Printed and bound in the
United States of America

Dedication

I believe that you have to *be* loved in order to *give* love. The Lord has blessed me with extraordinary parents. Their love has given me wings to fly my own journey and the security found in knowing the "nest" will always be wide open to welcome me.

There is no way I could have ever written about Jesus without first experiencing our loving Lord through the words, actions and lives of my parents.

When I was ordained, I had these words engraved on the base of my chalice. It is my privilege to repeat them here:

> My words will speak their praise,
>
> My eyes reflect their insight,
>
> My life will show their love,
>
> My faith was theirs at first.

In honor of Mom
and
In memory of Dad

Contents

So they took Jesus;
and carrying the cross by himself,
he went out to what is called

The Place of the Skull,
which in Hebrew is called
Golgotha.

There they crucified him,
and with him two others,
one on either side,
with Jesus between them.

John 19:16–18

He left the table and went into the
security of the familiar garden
called Gethsemane.

He had often sat and enjoyed
the beauty and peace
of this garden
outside the city of
Jerusalem.

But tonight was different.

He had often enjoyed
this haven of greenery,
the shade
of the twisted olive trees.

But tonight was different.

The power of the meal,
the gift of
body and blood
still pulsed in his heart.

He sought out
the huge rock
that jutted harshly
from the earth.

It stood in sharp contrast
to the garden.

Yet he was drawn to this altar of conflict.

His heart could hear his friends
leaving the Passover table asking
where he was.

His heart could hear the others
gathering
with clubs and torches.

But tonight was different.

A night of contrasts
a night of giving and being taken.

A night of celebrating
a night of humiliation.

A night of selfless sharing
a night of being bound and led away.

Slowly, he ascended
the rock in this garden
of Gethsemane.

His heart
torn between friends
and safety, mobs and madness.

But tonight was different.

He had to let evil triumph for a while,
mobs seemingly conquer
his mission as the
Word made Flesh.

Father, O Father,
take this cup from me.
Allow me the
safety and security
of this garden.

And the rock was spotted
with the blood of salvation
soon to be poured out
on the throne
of a cross.

Slowly
Insidiously
the noise of the crowd swelled
the evening grew darker
they came nearer.

And in his heart a voice...

Yes, Father,
your will be done.

Tonight is different.

He rose from the rock
to face his destiny
and the silent "yes"
watered the parched earth
and gardens bloomed.

The Adulterous Woman

"Woman,
where are they?
Has no one
condemned you?"

John 8:10

The Adulterous Woman

Why is it only in retrospect that we can see, with any clarity, our mistakes and our accomplishments, our feelings, and the reasons behind those feelings...

They burst through a fragile door and caught the two of us in bed. They crashed through our privacy and made my error public. As the door was splintered, I was blinded by the fire of their hatred. I clung to my partner, trying to shield myself from this burning, condemning hate. Hatred flourishes in the shallow ground of insecurity and blooms into the desire to impact another's life. Hatred flies like an arrow to a weak target. Hatred begins as thunder and then, when it joins with the hatred of others, bursts into flashes of lightning that strike out to sear and burn.

As I was thrown a robe and yanked through the broken door of my house, my partner walked out of the side door to resume his normal life. Two had committed sin, but only one was being publicly chastised. The penalty that these self-righteous people of thunder decided to impose on me for my sin was death by stoning.

The righteous are quick to preach that only God can forgive sin. Yet, how easily they decided I should die. There is something very wrong with a religion that allows no chance for redemption. I gave in to a moment of passion and the consequences were to be the stones that would tear my flesh and the accompaniment of jeers that would shred my heart.

As I was dragged through the town in which I grew up, my mind was racing and every fiber of my being screamed in terror and disbelief. The frenzied crowd pushing me to my execution grew with every step. Cowards, like leaves blowing in the wind, clustered to join in the condemnation of the powerless.

I don't know what hurt more, the men who were roughly pushing me to the spot where I would be stoned, or the women, with whom I shopped and chatted daily, who turned their backs and covered their children's eyes to keep them from looking at me.

There I was, half dressed and half crazy, being pulled to a horrible death. I had heard about stonings. My parents would tell me stories when I was a child. The men threw small stones first in order to inflict pain and then slowly increased the size of the stones so that death was not only inevitable, but as agonizing as possible.

I was never one who could tolerate pain. As a child, I would run to my mother with the smallest of cuts so she could kiss it, soothe it, and make the pain go away. Now, there was no one to make this pain go away.

Terror raced through my veins, stiffening my limbs, possessing my soul. I searched everywhere for a sign of compassion. I longed for a glimpse of my mother's face to banish this nightmare. I found only more thunder, roaring loudly from the eyes of the familiar yet foreign faces.

I was flung to the place where I was to die. My robe was in tatters. My emotions were in ruins. The place was totally devoid of life. No plant grew in the sand, and walls of stone surrounded me on three sides. But, the wall of humanity that filled the one open space made me realize that hatred was colder, harsher, more formidable than rocks.

They laughed at me. They taunted me. They burned my integrity with their words and their names. Though they claimed their actions in the name of religion, they acted as people who dwelled in darkness.

The Adulterous Woman

Everyone sins. Yet my sin was a public spectacle for those who considered themselves superior to me. I even saw my lover in the crowd, laughing and looking for stones.

The humiliation was so intense that I almost longed for the first stone to be thrown. How readily people become comrades when they are united in finding fault in the vulnerable. Just as thunder rolls and gathers, people of thunder converge. Seldom is there one to be found with the courage to stand in opposition to them. People are always afraid to stand up to thunder lest they get struck by lightning. I saw the faces of good people who had known me for all of my life, barely recognizable as they contorted with hatred and condemnation. I saw women with whom I had gathered water only this morning, now gathering stones to end my life. I saw men who had respected my family name now gleefully destroying my reputation. I saw pure hate. I saw sin greater than mine. What ripped away at my last thread of dignity was seeing children loosen rocks and bring them to the older men. How easily sin is passed on to the young as they try to imitate their elders, even in their wrong-doing.

Hopefully God would judge me with more mercy than these people who were my neighbors.

"Be quick with what you are about to do," was my only thought. The pain to come could not be worse than the pain that I was already experiencing. I felt that my personhood had already died. The stones would only complete the act by killing my body. My spirit had been dashed upon rocks of selfrighteousness and the jagged edges of others' judgements.

How I wished I could go back in time and not share my bed with that man. Life is that way. Caught up in a moment, we act in a manner we think is right, only later to wish we had acted differently. I couldn't help but wonder if these people, balancing the tools of my death in their hands, would feel the same after this moment of thunder passes.

Walking with Jesus

How I hated them all! The hate in my veins was the only thing that was keeping me steady at that moment. I tried to muster some dignity for my last moments of life, but everything had been stripped away from me. My mouth was filled with the dirt from this place where they so cruelly threw me. I wanted to stand up to meet their stones and their stony faces. Maybe I would even strike back with insults of my own. I had heard whispers about some of these people. I would die throwing my own stones at these hypocrites who were playing gods.

Suddenly, there was murmuring among them. They were arguing with someone, probably trying to add more energy to their thunder. I heard the muffled sounds of footsteps and the thuds of falling stones. I stood unsteadily on legs that seem made of water, poised to strike back. I was determined that my words would fly before their stones did. I decided to go out in my own moment of thunder.

But when I looked up, I was faced by a thunderless, gentle man whose eyes shone brighter than the searing sun. In the warmth of his eyes nothing burned but goodness and hope. Who was he and where did he come from? Would his words prove him, too, a person of thunder? He was holding a stick, a stick I imagined would be used for whipping me

The crowd seemed to be receding and dispersing—fading away into the harmless thunder that signals the end of a summer storm.

It seemed that we were the only two people in the world as this man asked me where the people who condemned me were. I wanted to scream out their names and rip the quiet air with tales of their past sinful deeds, but the unspoken words died in my throat. The dust from the earth choked any word of evil from my very being. He then said that he did not condemn me either.

Who was he? Where did this small man get such giant courage? What did he do or say to dispel the crowds of thunder?

The Adulterous Woman

He didn't know my name so he called me "woman." In his words I found the comfort of my mother kissing the hurt away. He quietly told me to sin no more. As gently as a branch moving in the morning air, he brushed away what others made into a carnival of accusation and anger. Who was this man? I only knew that what seemed like an end had been turned into a beginning.

As he left me, I slowly walked home to repair my door and my life. I wanted to restore the comfort of my home so that I could close the door and retreat from the world. Never again would I allow another man to enter my bed. Never again would I allow people to burst into the sanctuary of my home. Never again would I allow anyone to enter my life and control my feelings. I knew that his challenge would not be a problem—I would never commit that sin again. But I was filled with hatred and a need to avenge my shattered self-esteem.

I resumed my life as best I could. I felt that the only way I could survive was to return the hatred of my neighbors in an even stronger measure than they had given to me. Hate became the prime motivation in my life. It ruled my days and nights. Hate filled everything I did and possessed my entire being. I never missed an opportunity to resurrect a past scandal or start a new rumor. It amazed me that people who had turned their eyes away from me in their righteousness, now eagerly turned their ears toward me to hear the latest words of thunder that I gladly and hatefully spewed!

I existed only to pour out hate. Even in those quiet moments when I was alone in the bed where all of this had started, I thought of things to say, be they true or not, about those who took it upon themselves to condemn me. I vowed to give my last breath to the cause of ruining those who balanced stones in their hands. My days were as fierce as the storm of revenge that clouded my life. My days moved slowly as the crowd still shunned me, but individuals eagerly sought me out for the poison

I entertained them with. My words flashed out like lightning, striking at whomever I chose.

And so my days passed, days of deadly lightning, days of hatred and revenge.

Today something inexplicable drew me here to this hill, only to find myself here at the foot of the cross of him who stopped those who would have stoned me. I have been too busy to consider him much. How ironic to find myself here at his feet as his life drains away. Sadly enough, I was so engrossed in flashing lightning at those around me, that I allowed the very same lightning to blind me. I was so obsessed with the desire to hate that I never even bothered to find out my savior's name.

The intense light in his eyes is slowly fading as he is pummeled by the jeers and taunts of others. I am too late to save him from his fate. I wasn't even there to call out his name when the crowd chose who should live and who should die.

As I look around, I see some of the same people who had tried to stone me, now standing in this crowd. Some are taunting him, challenging him to come down from the cross and save himself. Hatred flares up in me again, hatred for those who did this to him. I try to give him some of my angry energy to sustain his life. "Hate them," I scream inside myself. "Hate them and make them disperse. Hate them and you will live!"

I start to turn away, knowing there is no way to save him. His eyes are closed now more than they are open. Suddenly he speaks. "Father, forgive them for they know not what they do."

Forgive them? Forgive them? No, hate them!! I turn to scream the words but am stopped by his thunderless face, his eyes of love, even as he hangs there in agony.

All at once the sky is filled with Godly thunder. In that moment I realize how wrong my hate is and how I have wasted my life dwelling in it. Suddenly I realize that he, whom I was trying to save, has once again saved me. I have been wasting my energy generating thunder. I have hidden the sun behind the storm clouds. As the rain pours down and his life is spent, I realize that though I had not committed that one sin again, I had committed many, many others. Now I must turn from those sins also.

As I walk home a different woman, I know that this man embodied a different choice for the days that we live. He was the thunderless prophet who spoke of the sun. He was the lightning rod that absorbed and diffused all of the lightning this world had to give.

I pass the place where they were to stone me. No longer is it a symbol to fuel hatred. Now I see in it a new way of living. Hatred has been replaced with love, love that begins with love, love that begins with forgiveness.

The thunderless prophet has banished my thunder.

Lazarus

*...[Jesus] cried with a loud voice,
"Lazarus, come out!" The dead man
came out, his hands and feet bound with
strips of cloth, and his face wrapped
in a cloth. Jesus said to them,
"Unbind him, and let him go."*

John 11:43–44

Lazarus

He was my friend. Martha and Mary were gifts granted to me through birth, but the gift of Jesus I chose myself. The ability to choose a friend is a true blessing from the Almighty. Friendship is a powerful bond between hearts. It is through friends that we experience most clearly the Creator's love on earth.

Jesus was unlike anyone I had ever known. His vision never seemed firmly focused in the here and now. He wasn't tied down to this world by things. He never owned anything, but, at the same time, everything was his. Looking back, all of nature seemed to reach out to catch his words when he spoke. The very stones seemed to strain to hear him. Flowers seemed to preen their glorious blooms when he walked by. Birds quieted their perpetual chirping when they heard his voice. All of the world was caught in his power and gave him respect.

I didn't see my friend Jesus too often. I knew that he had to be about a mission. True friendship is never possessive or controlling. We lived our separate lives and rejoiced at the times we shared.

Those hours we spent together seemed to fly by. They never seemed long enough. We talked about all kinds of things, both earthly and heavenly. We didn't always agree, but that never stood between us. He had an air of gentle intensity about him. He knew the fullness of life. He had mountain-top vision but deep in his eyes was the shadow of an untouchable sadness. And when that sadness came more to the fore, he would go away. Even though he existed to touch humanity, there were times he needed to be alone. Although he lived to fill people with a new sense of life, death was constantly at his back. His detractors made sure of that!

I knew that he would get in trouble with the religious leaders. He was not a person obsessed by rules and regulations. He lived by what he taught. Our religion had become too staid and too rigid. In essence, we had lost our humanness and our need.

When I lay dying, I knew I would see him again. I knew this with my very soul. But in the end, death came to me before he did. He was far distant, busy with his mission when I breathed my last breath and entered into a new plane of existence.

I had always feared death. It was a fear that I had discussed many times with my friend Jesus. He talked to me about a life after death. My friend became my mentor. My friend became my hope. He removed my fear. Through his love, I knew that there was nothing to fear, even after death.

As death covered me like the fog that gently creeps over a countryside, my vision cleared. I watched as they anointed my body with balm but could not smell its pungent aroma. I saw them wrapping my body in linens but felt nothing. I watched as they placed my body in a tomb and rolled the stone over the entrance.

I saw, but did not hear, the wails of my sisters, Martha and Mary, until the stone blocked out everything. Even through all this, my heart was confident that I would see my friend Jesus again, and I was quite content to wait for his arrival.

The darkness of death was broken by a gentle light that called my essence back into my body. Suddenly I became aware of the linens that were binding me and felt the cold, dampness of the tomb in which I lay. Slowly, awkwardly, I stumbled through the now open mouth of the cave of death where I had lain, answering the call of my long-awaited friend. The cloths that bound my body were removed, just as he had removed bindings from my inner being time and time again.

When my eyes blinked away death, I saw his face. He was smiling a self-knowing smile that I had seen in my heart before I died. My heart leapt when I saw my friend once again. After my reawakening, I knew and understood, more clearly than most, what he was all about.

My heart knew, from that day when he brought me back to life, that Jesus would soon get into tremendous trouble. He seemed to turn his sights on our leaders and wanted to shake the dust of death from their beliefs and rules. That was a very risky business!

During the time we spent together after that day, we spoke very little. When Jesus would visit, we would just sit with each other. True friends never need an abundance of words. He would look at me and just give me a small nod of his head, knowing that I knew. I knew who he was. I knew what he was all about. I knew that he was a person of life who banished death to the furthest, darkest corner of our existence. And my heart trembled as I also knew that the bolder he became with his challenge to the people and to our leaders, the more they would turn against him

I still don't know why people choose death over life or darkness over light, but they do. People are afraid to let themselves be loved. People fear change and goodness. Goodness tends to be squashed more quickly than an insect walking on a path! People welcome days of death rather than life. People will do everything in their power to avoid dying but spend most of their days embracing death and giving death to others. We are such stubborn people when it comes to really living life!

Jesus showed me that most people live only a pale shadow of life. When my friend talked about life, he used words like "fullest" and "abundance." He made me see that life is an endless stream of clear, cleansing water that too many people just stand on the banks, content to watch it flow by. Jesus lived each day by taking risks. He challenged people to move beyond the self-imposed death of "can't" into a realm of actualization, of grace and mercy and love. People need to leap into the arms of my friend Jesus, not stop, think, analyze, and then reconsider!

What did my friend Jesus do to bring himself death? He forgave people. He gave people a second chance at living life. He healed anyone who expressed their need. He fed the hungry with food that could be found no where else on this earth. He removed the boulders of guilt that burdened down people who believed what others wanted them to. He brushed the dust from people who lived under the feet of others and made them stand erect. He took those shunned by the self-righteous and gave them self-respect. He gently washed away the "no, I can't" from people's hearts and replaced them with "yes, I can." He took people from the rocky crags and set them on the tree-lined road of a love-filled journey. In return they gave him a taste of what he had stood in opposition to—death itself.

I stayed close to him during his lasts weeks on this earth, quiet and unnoticed in his shadow. I saw the throngs throw their cloaks and wave palms when he entered the city. It was a crowd spurred on by the emotion of the moment. They were not strong believers following the dictates of changed hearts. I knew they would turn against him like the unpredictable wind. On that day that everyone was calling "triumphant," I saw in his eyes a look that was distant and removed, while at the same time focused and determined. I knew on that day he entered the city we call "holy" that it was not true holiness in people that was surfacing. The palms themselves were stronger in their love of life than those who waved them. People are quick to follow something new but few remain loyal when inner change is asked. It is easier to band with death than walk alone in the light of life. I saw the look on the leaders' faces when he entered our city. They were like spoiled children being asked to give their favorite toy to another child.

Lazarus

I was not surprised when my friend Jesus was arrested like a common criminal. They had to throw mud on him who made the desert bloom. They had to trump up charges against him. I knew their words would sway some who had followed Jesus. Some would abandon him and leave him to die alone.

I knew that the bearers of death would do everything in their power to restore things to the way they were before Jesus came and taught and shared. I knew that they thought in killing him they could stamp out the new life that had begun to sprout in so many.

It came as no surprise to me that they screamed for Barabbas over Jesus. The bearers of death did their work well. So strong is death's smothering grip that people slip back into it as quickly and easily as they change their clothes. When death grabs at one's heart, the choice to live withers. And so many of those very people to whom Jesus had given life were the ones screaming for Barabbas.

Someday this day will be looked on as one of glory because of what his pain and death will bring. I suffer pain with my friend because through love, pain is always shared. We shared death before. I know that the death of his body will not be the end of him. He will return. He spoke of it openly to closed ears and hearts. The truth cannot be stopped by whips or crosses, by rumors and false accusations. Truth is life to those who believe.

I decide to leave before his life drains from his body. I do not want to see him still and cold. As I turn to go, I see him raise his head and hear him utter "Father forgive them for they know not what they are doing."

How true, my friend, how true! They know not what they are doing, not just with today's actions but every time someone chooses a moment of death over a chance to live.

I smile at him and nod, trying to imitate that same self-knowing look that I saw when my own bandages were removed. I walk away and turn my back on another moment of death, the death of my friend Jesus.

The Writer

*"Come to me
all you that are weary
and are carring heavy burdens,
and I will give you rest."*

Matthew 11:28

The Writer

He never knew me by name, but he knew the very fiber of my being. That is more important than knowing what we are called. Names can easily change, but fibers must grow, nurtured by the prodding of another.

I have given my life to words. I have written and rewritten them. I have constructed thoughts into images. I have allowed others to feel through the experience of the written word. Words can give life and words can rob life. That choice is ours each time we open our mouths or put pen to paper.

Everyone appreciates the written form, though most are frightened by the content. Such was the case with Jesus. He was more than just a weaver of words. When he spoke, the words seemed new and fresh. When words rolled from his lips, you knew they began in his heart. When words seek out and lodge in your heart, then you know, beyond explaining, that they are authentic.

We are a people filled with high ideals, but those ideals wither as quickly as flowers cut in the noon day sun when they are not practiced in our daily lives.

Every person needs honesty in his or her life. Every person longs for affirmation as surely as a traveler in the desert longs for a cool spring. Every person follows a light that seems so distant. When I heard the words of Jesus, I knew that the light had drawn near. Here was the One for whom generations had been waiting.

Most people step into life wanting to change the world, only to wake up one morning and find the world has changed them. Jesus spoke with a fire of change, personal change. Worlds do not change. People do. But in people changing, the world becomes different.

His words testified that he was the Promised One. Our world had grown old. He spoke and showed us that regardless of the age-lessness of the world, no one had to be old. His words spurred dreams and dreams keep us alive and young. A world without dreams is a desert. A person without dreams is dead.

The easiest place to hide is within your very self. Many had become too comfortable with speaking the right words but living the wrong way. Jesus had the simple power to expose the true self within each one of us and by his words taught us to love what we rediscovered. We strive for love yet create reasons to hate. We invent reasons to fight but hide from the power of loving. We laugh at death and boldly claim that we are not ready. How preposterous that we cling to what is not ours while ignoring everything that is truly ours to enjoy and share. We say we love to think yet we let others kill our ideas. We say we are good people yet we turn away when others are dying the many deaths we face each day. We say we are religious yet we never live a life of faith.

No wonder he turned to the prostitutes, the tax collectors and the sinners. They were the people who were still needy enough to allow God to improvise with them.

Words can make us understand our existence because they unlock the limitless possibilities of the person we are called to become. Jesus opened so many lives with his words. He was different from any other person that had ever uttered words. Jesus spoke, not to hear the echo of his own voice, but the echo of his words in the voices of others.

When he would speak with outstretched arms, a living bridge was formed. As one traveled over that bridge, one experienced his heart and found the bridge between heaven and earth.

I stand here listening to him; he is bound to the wood, yet still speaking words. He is using every opportunity to speak what the world had always known but never before heard.

He dies and the words stop. However, their ringing still echoes within the chambers of my being. I am sure that I am not alone. Now he, who taught us that we spend too much time protecting empty graves rather than venturing out into the light, will be placed in a cold, dark tomb, but his echoes will resound for generations to come.

Although we can forget how a flower looks, can we ever forget the smell? And if we ever forget what bread looks like, would we ever forget the taste? We may forget what this Jesus looked like, but we will never forget his words....They are firmly planted in the soil of our hearts. We now must be his voice and repeat those same words for different ears to hear!

The Ten Lepers

"…Were not ten made clean?
But the other nine, where are they?
Was none of them found
to return and give praise to God
except this foreigner?"

Luke 17:17–18

The Ten Lepers

The realization of my lack of gratitude drew me here to this place. The "Skull Place"—an apt name. Here amidst strewn bones and broken dreams people are brought to be punished. Here criminals and innocent family are bonded together by fear, pain, and loss of personal power. But from today on, this place will become known for all of history. The Skull Place will henceforth be remembered as a place of power and life.

I was young when I realized that my skin was rotting away. I was sent away from my home and told that I would have to wear a bell around my neck and scream for others to get out of my way, lest they become infected. I was made to feel as if I was the scourge of the human race.

One day, walking down a road so familiar that it seemed as much a home as any I had ever known, a band of fellow lepers and I heard a clamor that overpowered even our bells. The man, purported to be the long-awaited one was coming. A new day was being heralded in with his arrival. People were proclaiming him the Messiah. So, in the same way we usually cried out for bread or a few tossed coins, we now cried out for mercy and healing.

It's hard to say if any of us screamed out of real belief or just out of the off chance that the fanatical rumors happened to be true. We were not people to let any opportunity pass us by. What would this man do? How would he react to a band of dirty, smelly lepers? Would he veer from the road and avoid us as mistakes of nature? Would he come and bestow on us some words dripping with sentiment and false hope? Would he toss us some token coins and thus cleanse himself of the guilt of being whole? I didn't know what to expect. This was the first time that I had ever crossed paths with a "Messiah."

Surprisingly, he did not veer away from us. Nor did he hesitate. Instead, he approached us aglow with an acceptance and love that I had never experienced before. He asked us what we wanted of him. To be made whole, of course, was the unanimous answer from this band of ten lepers. He smiled at us as if our request was a simple one. And with his smile, the healing began.

In body parts that had reeked with rot, new life was beginning. As I could feel my skin crawl with the new life, my heart began to race and warm light burst throughout my skull.

We stood there like children, speechless at receiving a gift wonderful beyond imagining. Though our exteriors still looked the same, we knew in our hearts that we had been blessed with new life and a second chance at living.

He spoke again and told us to wash and then go and present ourselves to the priest. We were stunned and overwhelmed as we went to do what he asked.

As we bathed, the water washed away not only our rotting outsides, but also cleansed our insides. With every splash of water inner scars were purged from our bodies. As the old water mixed with the new in the flowing river, my eyes were also clearing and finding a new perspective on living. Washed away was powerlessness. Washed away was the feeling of not belonging and the hurt and loneliness of not being accepted. My body and soul were cleansed in the living water that wondrous day.

We emerged from the water and, with all the strength our healed limbs could muster, we hurled our hated bells as far as we could. As we began to walk, we were taken aback by the silence—the joyful, peaceful silence—no bells, no clanging. We went to the priest to fulfill the second part of our healer's request. I will never forget the look on his face, as the priest—the one who shunned us and shackled us with our tell-tale bells—realized who we were. We all stood in silence—the priest, stunned, and we, whole lepers, defiant. We turned to leave and found that for the first time in many years, we were laughing, giddy with our reentry into the human race.

We argued joyfully about what to do next. There was so much of life that we had been forced to miss. Nine of us wanted to see and experience, taste and feel. One did not take part in the wild planning and quietly went his separate way.

The glory of living totally for myself lasted only for a while. Self-centered living, doing, seeing, and experiencing satisfied my head, but not my heart.

The nine of us soon parted company and went our own ways. I kept looking back to that momentous day and was haunted by the question asked—what do I want. Something was missing. The answer always seemed just outside my grasp.

One day, I met up with the one cured leper who had slipped quietly away from our band. He told me that he had returned to the source of healing and simply said, "Thank you." Then it struck me—that was where the missing part of my life was to be found.

I searched in vain for that man whom I had met on the road. As often happens in life, when you are purposefully searching for something, it eludes you.

It was Passover. I came to the Holy City to celebrate something I was never before allowed to. It was there I found the familiar face, branded a criminal. He was there hanging on a cross. I did not know what had happened to him or how his life had led him here. I had been so busy living my life the way I wanted that I had lost track completely of the one who had given me new life.

I walked to the Skull Place feeling as if I had been here before. Not this particular plot of land, but a similar place where I had been crucified by feelings of bitterness, anger, envy, and pride. I walked on stones that I had long ago dropped from my heart. I walked and approached him whom others were turning away from.

Our roles were now reversed. He was the leper and I was whole. Although he did not wear a bell, he now wore a cross to declare his shame. He was the one who cried out alone. He was the one that people turned their eyes away from. He, in all his power, was now powerless in the face of many.

As I approached him, I regretted that I did not have the authority within to tell him to wash himself and all would be well. I felt the same burning in my heart and the same crawling in my skin that I had felt that fateful day on the road. I approached him to utter two words, long overdue.

Things were happening so fast; the scene almost seemed carnival-like in its unreality. Soldiers were gambling for his clothes. The air vibrated with sounds, some jeering and some wailing. The priests were screaming something about invoking Elijah. Their words were hollow echoes as I ventured closer, ever closer. Old feelings were assailing me as I walked toward him on legs that he had healed. Soldiers blocked my path. No one looked at me or away from me, for all eyes were on him. Holy man. Healing man. Broken man. Friend.

For one second that stopped the very motion of the earth, he looked at me. Now was my time. I uttered those words that completed my healing process. As a partner in pain, I said from my heart, "Thank you." Immediately after I voiced those words, he gazed to the heavens and said, "It is completed."

The earth shook and the heavens opened. He didn't have to go to the water to wash and be made whole. As the heavens opened, the water came to him and washed his body there on the cross. I looked down and noticed his blood mingling with his water of healing surrounding my feet. I did not move, but allowed myself to be bathed once again in his life.

An Unidentified Man

*And they were filled with great awe
and said to one another,
"Who then is this, that even the
wind and the sea
obey him?"*

Mark 4:41

An Unidentified Man

Passover—the time for my yearly visit to the temple. Since time is money, and organization one of the guiding forces in my life, I arrived in Jerusalem early to avoid the crowds. I always make sure I can visit the temple and still have enough time to do some business on the side. The time for sacrificing lambs is a perfect opportunity to make some business contacts. Now, having finished both duty and business, I prepare to leave early, before the actual holiday. As I near the city gates on my way home, I see a large crowd at a crucifixion and I curse the time I will lose getting through the mob.

There are three men on crosses. I give them a cursory glance and suddenly I am struck by the realization that the face in the middle is one I know. (I never forget a face—it's so important in business.)

As I work my way through the crowd, my mind goes back to the two times our paths crossed. The first time must have been about three years ago. I remember because it was around the time I first started feeling the turmoil within me.

I prided myself in always being in control of my life. I usually accomplished what I set out to do. I could organize my day, my household, and my family. (Days move faster when one knows what has to be done.)

But one day I woke up and began to wonder why I wanted my days to move faster. Where were they leading me? What would the

end result be? What did I ultimately hope to accomplish? I knew I had to solve my own problems in life—it was the only way they would be taken care of. But my life seemed so empty and incomplete. It was like there was a piece missing inside that was crying out to be put into place.

This country has always been known for producing good fruit, hot days and false prophets. I was never very interested in hearing these men with their self-serving messages about how to live and who to love and hate. But sometimes I found myself searching them out, looking for refreshing water, only to be given words that passed like sand in the wind.

Then one day I heard about this man named John, who would stand in the water and baptize people, telling them to prepare, change and reform. Something about this message, trite as it was, appealed to me. Maybe this man would hold the key. Maybe something in his words could quiet that nagging need inside me. Maybe he would be the one...

So, I journeyed to the Jordan to see this John. Some called him a madman, some a prophet, but I withheld all judgment, wanting to decide for myself. (I have always been able to make clear, definite decisions about people I meet.)

When I arrived at the Jordan, there were a lot of people ahead of me waiting to get water poured over their heads. So many, in fact, that I became annoyed. I knew I should have given myself more time to get there. I could have been in the front of the line rather than wasting time waiting.

I started to talk to the person in front of me. I did the polite thing—introduced myself and told him a little about myself—but what do you do after you have exhausted the normal pleasantries? I did what everyone else does and started to complain: The line was too long; I hoped the water wasn't too cold; why was John taking so long with each person; he ought to have some helpers to keep people in line and keep it moving. I babbled on and on.

He listened and only smiled. He never shared anything about himself or commented on my minor complaints. "Well!" I thought. "If he wants to be alone and quiet, then so be it!"

And so we moved at a snail's pace getting deeper and deeper into the murky water and coming closer and closer to John. Since that strange fellow in front of me wasn't interested in polite, everyday conversation, and there wasn't anything better to do, I began to watch John. He seemed so determined and vehement with his message. He was actually shouting about sins and the need to change.

Finally it was his turn—my reticent neighbor in line. The fierce and raging John of moments before suddenly became very docile and obviously distracted. He was refusing to baptize that man. I strained to hear what they were saying but the ripples in the water seemed to get louder, blocking out my hearing.

I figured that this man must have been filled with sin if John was refusing to pour water on his head. I tried to catch what they were saying, hoping to have some real gossip to share when I reached the drying off place on the other bank.

Dear God in heaven! I hoped that John wouldn't refuse me too. Maybe he knew I had been complaining in line. More likely, I decided, he was getting bored with all of these people and was looking for a way to get through this endless line.

But wait. It seemed that John decided to baptize the man after all. "Good," I thought as I realized I was next. I hoped this John didn't take as much time with me as he did with that other fellow. I had much left to do that day. I was getting anxious because I was aware that my schedule was slipping.

As I began edging forward, trying to hurry things along, everything suddenly seemed to stand still. The water seemed to quiet and the earth seemed to jolt. I remember thinking it odd, perhaps a sudden earthquake. Unexpectedly, the clouds parted and the sun got brighter.

At that point, I thought I heard a voice coming from the heavens, but decided that it was probably thunder or someone's voice bouncing off of the mountains. (I remember thinking how strange—earthquakes and thunder. It seemed the wrong time of year and we hadn't had the slightest warning.)

"Move along, man!" I wanted to urge the man in front of me. I wanted to get this done and get on with my life! I had so many important things to do and I would have to postpone a lot of my tasks until the next day if this took much longer.

Finally! My turn! But this resolute John now seemed distracted, even shaken. He rushed me through in a flash. I didn't see what the big deal was. I didn't feel any different. It had been a total waste of my time.

I went home annoyed at myself for squandering so much time. After all, time is money and wasted time is missed opportunities. I had really made a mess of that day! I had to rearrange my schedule. I was a very busy man, much busier than most people realize. Never again would I waste a whole day on dreams.

I saw this same man again some time later. I was on a short trip across the Sea of Galilee. Again I was waiting—this time for a boat to take me from one side of the lake to the other. I had some important business to do on the other side and not much time.

He was getting into a boat with some scruffy men. By the look of the company he was keeping, John's message hadn't had any effect on him either. Like I said, I never forget a face. Ever the cordial person, I waved and said to him that it was too bad about what had happened to John. (He was killed, you know.) I only said it because it was the proper thing to do. Inwardly I felt John was just another false prophet and got what he deserved.

Both of the boats we rode in started out at the same time. Looking at the sky and the calmness of the water, I predicted the trip would be smooth and quick. Much to my surprise, when we were about halfway across, a storm hit. It was totally unexpected and furious in intensity. A few of the others sharing the boat with me were becoming very afraid. My own distress came more from the precious minutes I was losing and my daily schedule being thrown off. As I held on for dear life, I glanced over at the other boat. It was being tossed around like a child's toy, and there, in the midst of it all, was that man, sound asleep. (What was it with him and the weather?) I became indignant.

I decided it was not good for me to be near this man. He was bringing me trouble again, making me late once more.

I looked over at his boat again, and, to my surprise, he was standing up. This is a very foolish thing to do in such a raging storm. As the winds and rains seemed to intensify even more, he stretched out his arms and muttered something. Much to my astonishment, the storm suddenly stopped. I had never seen that happen before. I thought I should really catch up with him when we reached the shore and ask him about his little act and how he made people believe he stopped the storm. If I could learn his tricks, I could impress a lot of people. Think of how much better I could plan each day if I could conquer the weather! But when we reached the shore, I was very aware of how late I was, so I rushed off to do my business...

And now we meet a third time, and yet again he is making me late! All these people jeering and gawking, blocking the road.

I knew he was going to go wrong. He didn't have the polish and conversational skills to get involved in everyday politics or business. Maybe I should go up to him and advise him in the error of his ways, but then it would probably be rubbing salt in his wounds. And what's the sense now anyway? Besides, my time is precious and is quickly slipping away. Even though I had gained some extra time by getting an early start, I was now going to be late.

At least the weather is on my side. The day couldn't be more beautiful. My journey home would be easy in this balmy weather. Suddenly I feel the earth jolt again as I did in the Jordan, only this time the jolt feels angry as if someone is shaking a naughty child.

I don't believe it! It's suddenly dark and raining. Where did these clouds come from? Again this man and the weather! I should have known! I glance over to him in anger because I know this poor weather is his fault. But he is dead. When I look at his face this time, I feel my inner world tremble. Instead of the earth shaking, my very soul is shaking. My vision of an organized and controlled life now seems cloudy. I feel all that I have organized in my life now dropping as insignificantly as the rain. All of this because of looking at his face.

Did he somehow hold the missing pieces to the puzzle of my life? Could he have been what I have been looking for? Could he have made me feel complete? What a ridiculous thought! How could that be? This pitiable man wound up like John. Poor soul, he never understood what it meant to fit in with life.

I shake the feeling from me and then become angry with myself for wasting so much time. I have work to do, people to see and things to get done. On with my life! I am already behind schedule!

This entire episode is just another inconvenience to complain about when I get home. At least I will have someone to blame my tardiness on.

I give him one last look and make myself overlook my inner trembling. Be in control once again, I tell myself. Stick to what you know has to be done. Be determined and organized and things in life fall into place. Ignore this interior quaking. People may notice and see it as a sign of weakness and one must always be strong.

I start again on my journey home. I begin to grumble to the men walking beside me. I introduce myself and then complain about Passover crowds and the increase of prices of sacrificial lambs. At least they answer me.

I look back one last time at this man's face and think to myself...at least I don't have to worry about the weather!!

The Mother of Judas

*When Judas,
his betrayer, saw that
Jesus was condemned,
he repented and brought back
the thirty pieces of silver to the
chief priests and the elders.*

Matthew 27:3

The Mother of Judas

My son died today, too. I loved him like every mother loves her child. When I cradled my baby in my arms, I imagined the countless possibilities and journeys of his future. I saw nothing but bright horizons and limitless potential. But all of that was cut short—my son died by his own hand.

When I was told he was dead, a part of me died, too. Facing how he died took more strength than I thought I could ever muster. Sharing pain is part of parenting, but it is a part that is shared more intensely by a mother. Bearing a child into the world forges indelible and everlasting ties that run deeper than most people know.

Just as he died alone, so I buried Judas alone. There was no commotion, no gathering of mourners. It was a very solitary act. I looked at his face one last time and my heart screamed the unanswerable question, "Why?"

Oh, I hear the whispers of others. They murmur words about Judas that pierce my very soul. I hear words like "traitor" and "back-stabber."

One of the hardest things for a mother to do is to let her children go. We try to shield our children from the inevitable bumps and bruises. We try to make sure that they avoid the pitfalls of life, but to no avail.

I always wanted the best for my son. Although I saw his weaknesses and flaws, I always tried to make him realize his potential.

But what other people thought of him was too important to Judas. He needed to be needed. He wanted to be recognized and known. He wanted to be important. Today I think his name and his importance died with him.

Judas was driven. He was never content with what was. He always wanted more and more and more. There was never sufficient time in a day for my son. Regardless of all he accomplished, he would look at the setting sun and think of all that had yet to be done. This caused my son to be in constant inner turmoil. Judas had a raging fire within him, a fire which eventually caused his demise. That inner fire scorched and seared his good points as he challenged the concept that life can never be conquered or controlled.

As I watched him grow, I saw more and more a child in chaos. A person who desires so desperately to be known needs to hide his or her true self. He did so much, but showed so little feeling. He displayed a passionless passion for achieving his goals. Judas had a good heart, but he kept it very well hidden. He would cry, but cry alone. He could love deeply but would not let it be seen. He could feel with great sensitivity, but buried that, considering it a sign of weakness.

Judas was a loner. I never knew Judas to be part of the crowd. He needed to control and influence the crowd, to move it to where he wanted it to be, but never be a part of it. He could charm people with his words and mesmerize them like a swaying cobra. People listened to my son. That was the problem. He said the right words but they lacked true feeling. They were bones without flesh.

Judas was a natural leader. That was why I was so stunned when he told me that he was leaving home and the future he had planned to become a follower of Jesus.

Yet I came to believe he had found himself in those years with Jesus. Word would come back to me about how happy he was. When he would return home for short visits, I saw a new son. As Judas would share all of the things Jesus was preaching and doing,

I would see a new fire in his eyes. But sometimes when I would talk to him, I would see his eyes move again to that far-away place. I knew that the closer my son was to allowing his real self to shine through, the more turmoil he was in. It is a very hard thing for a man to allow himself to be who he truly knows he is.

I listened intently to the stories that Judas shared and kept quiet about the change I saw in my son. I watched and waited to see if his true self would emerge. During his last visit, he talked little and stared much. He kept mentioning the growing darkness of confusion stirring within him. Try as I would, I could not lift this despair from my son. A mother's frustration is the only thing that surpasses a mother's pain. I hated seeing my son in turmoil. I feared the fact that I could not reach him. A nameless fury and desperation clawed at my insides.

Judas had never been honest with those closest to him, those who really knew him. I am not sure why children feel that they cannot be honest with their parents. We already know the truth about those to whom we have given birth and have watched grow, but we need to hear that truth before we can intercede. I never got to hear those words of truth from my son Judas, although I tried my hardest to pry them from him.

I remember his agitation during his last visit home. He kept babbling on and on about Jesus not being the "One." He kept rambling on about changing sides and taking matters into his own hands. His words scared me and caused me many sleepless nights. I was truly frightened for my son.

What happened from there I do not know. All I know is that my son is dead. I went and took his body and brought it home. How long has it been since he really rested in this home? Now he will rest forever—close by my side.

On my slow, grief-filled journey home, I passed the mother of Jesus. She was on a mission similar to mine. Her son had died, too, and I feared that my son had somehow played a part in it. I dreaded meeting her, for I knew she would hate me for the sins of my child. Though I tried to avoid her, we ended up face to face. I braced myself for a torrent of words that would lash out at me, although my pain was already so deep I didn't think I could be hurt any more. I said nothing, trying to keep the meeting between us as short as possible. I needed to bury my son. She needed to bury her son. We were two mothers bound together by the deaths of our first born children.

I know that the hands of many nailed her son to a tree, but already voices were rising to blame my Judas. The others who stood idly by and allowed him to be killed should share in the blame. The forgotten many share in the guilt of the blood deeds acted out by a remembered few. Still, I struggled at the approach of Jesus's mother.

As we faced one another on that road, time seemed to stand still. I waited for her to scream at me, almost wanting her to spill out the emotion I knew she must be feeling. But instead of lashing out, she simply bowed her head and nodded to me, a sharer of pain. In that nod I recognized a woman blessed. In that nod, I sensed a mother for the whole world. In that nod, I felt that she shared my grief. No malice or hatred or blame accompanied it. There was just a consoling nod that said we were partners in pain, friends at separate funerals, and women who were no longer called on to nurse their children.

Our sons were very different. Both had their ideas and both had their dreams. Both died on the same day. Both died in different ways for different reasons. I am sure that many will remember her son. I only hope that my Judas, who so wanted to be known and remembered, will be seen not as a villain, but as one who made a final mistake. Her son spoke so freely about forgiveness; will that forgiveness be extended to my son?

Memory is choosing what and how we want to remember. I will always love my son. I tried my best to nurture the good in him and to enable him to be himself. I buried my son, but not my memories of the child I knew and loved.

The Owner of the Room of the Last Supper

[Jesus] said, "Go into the city to a certain man, and say to him, 'The Teacher says, My time is near; I will keep the Passover at your house with my disciples.'"

Matthew 26:18

The Owner of the Room
of the Last Supper

I have managed to make my living by renting my room. It is a fine room with a lot of airy space that most find desirable. The location couldn't be better. It is not right in the Holy City so it does not have a lot of noise and distraction. My room is nestled on a small hill and is distant yet close.

There have been all sorts of celebrations in my room. People have gathered to laugh, to celebrate, to mourn, to comfort and to forget what life is all about.

Passover time is usually a slow time since most are home with their families. Few people need to rent a room that they do not call their own for the holy day.

But that Passover, my room was not empty. I have never had a more unusual bunch than those twelve men and their leader. I hesitated about renting to them at first because I did not know whether or not his reputation would hurt my business. But then, I decided, a booking is a booking, and money is money, regardless of whose it is.

When I inquired what they would like to dine on, I was informed that they wanted the traditional Passover meal. Few people realize the work involved in preparing the many different meals people request and trying to please everyone's tastes. I was relieved that this group was not fussy nor concerned with details.

Walking with Jesus

One of the joys I find in what I do is gathering stories with which I can entertain my friends. I eavesdrop a lot. Usually when the wine starts to flow freely, the tales get more and more interesting....

This gathering did not look promising in that aspect. The men came together in a subdued mood. The leader seemed almost distracted. The meal was quiet and peaceful, the participants somehow distant yet cohesive. One person seemed uncomfortable and fidgeted a lot, but since he was the one who held the money, I overlooked his apparent uneasiness.

That night my wife came along to help with the meal. As we served them, we moved quickly and quietly, enabling them to have enough privacy and at the same time, feed my curiosity.

All bowed their heads low when the traditional opening prayer began—all except the one in charge of the money. He seemed to glare at their leader with a combination of anger and awe. Their leader used the customary words of the Passover meal. He did everything with such care that it almost seemed that this would be his last time doing it. I wondered if he was going away.

Then, as my wife and I stood back waiting for them to finish the meal, their leader began to make up different words. It might sound strange, but as he shared the bread and wine, he talked as if he were sharing his very self. Then he began to talk about his death. Can you think of a quicker way to ruin a party, not that this one was very jovial, than to speak about death, especially your own?

The expressions on the other men's faces ranged from fear to awe to very intense love. Their eyes never left his as they passed around the bread and shared the cup. I held my breath, fearing something would spill on my floor.

However, something very strange seemed to happen as they ate the bread and sipped the wine. These grown men took on the look of children who have found the missing piece of a puzzle—a piece that they thought was lost. The demeanor of these big, towering men changed, all except one.

The youngest of the group even laid his head on the chest of their leader. It was a tender, loving gesture, and one that spoke of great trust. They all seemed to relax around the table and their conversation became very soft. I tried to get closer to hear better what they were talking about, but before I could, there was a sudden commotion and upheaval. Indignant cries, something about betrayal, swept through the group like a fire fanned by the wind. Only the one with the purse seemed apart from it.

The leader gently pushed the young one aside and took another piece of bread. He dipped it into the dish at the same time the one who holds the money did. There was a sudden hush. A look of sadness crept over the young one's face and a look a relief came over the leader.

Once again a commotion arose and the one who was supposed to pay me got up from the table. The leader told him to "do what he had to do and do it quickly." Foolishly I assumed that he meant paying me for the room, but he pushed his way right past me and looked back one last time at the leader. My wife gave me a look that screamed, "Stop him!"—but I knew there was no stopping him. I never saw a more tormented look on a man's face than I did when he left the room. It frightened me to see so much darkness in a person's face. I tried to stay calm. I thought he'd be back. Who would leave such a nice room and such good friends?

As the uproar died down, the men seemed to be getting quite sleepy. I hoped it was the sleepiness of the contented after a fine meal. Usually that means an extra little bit of money when the bill is paid.

They began to move toward the cool garden that is nearby. The garden is well known for its beautiful trees and the fine olives they produce. Many people pass by it and miss its beauty. I usually try to tell my clients about the garden so that they can stroll through it and digest some of the fine food that my wife prepared. Most people never listen, but rather hurry back to their busy lives.

They all walked right past me—their leader too. I felt my wife's stare again and knew I should try to stop him—yet I could not. As I stood there and watched him move into the garden, my heart told me that he would return.

As I turned back to the emptiness of the room, reality slapped me in the face. My wife's voice, as gentle as stones being scraped together, reminded me of the need we have to pay our bills and feed our family. I usually ask for payment ahead of time, but there seemed to be little thought for that when the men came to rent my room. Something inside of me knew I had to rent it to them, and somehow I forgot to ask for the money beforehand.

Giving into my wife's words, or maybe just escaping her shrill tones, I left all of the dirty dishes for her to clean and followed them into the garden. I found most of the men had fallen asleep, faster than they should have. They had shared a Passover meal and not a lot of wine, so I was surprised that sleep would have over-taken them so quickly.

I walked further and saw their leader on the top of a big rock He was in deep contemplation. Out of respect, I didn't get too close. I heard him say something about the "cup passing from him." Surely he couldn't have been referring to the meal I had just served him!

I went back and looked among the sleeping ones for the one holding the purse. He was not there. I told myself he would prob-ably join them later. None of them made any secret of their desti-nation at the end of dinner. No one seemed in a hurry to be going anywhere, except maybe the leader and the one holding the money, but they both seemed to be going in very different directions.

Everything began happening very quickly. I heard the clamor of men with a vile purpose. I became quite fearful. I wondered if they were coming to seek out the leader who was just coming down from the rock. He had tiny drops of blood on his face. I wondered if he scraped himself as he came off of the rock. I relaxed a bit when I saw the one with the purse leading the mob. But as he got closer and I saw his face, my blood turned to ice water. The anger of all of humanity was clearly outlined on his intent, flint-hard face. I became very confused when I saw him go up and kiss the leader's face as if he hadn't seen him in a long time.

The sleeping followers awoke. I ran from the garden. I felt uneasy about what I had seen. I rushed to the security of my wife, only to hear her bleating about the money, the money, the room, the room. I needed quiet to think about what I had seen but she gave me no peace. Her incessant harping continued until at last I faked sleep just to get some peace. I hoped that by the next day she would forget the entire episode and let me go on with my life. Such was not to be the case.

As soon as the rooster beckoned the morning, she began again with her tirade about what was owed us. I knew that there would be no peace until I tried once again to get the money for the room.

I walked into the chaos of the city at Festival time. People were rushing to buy sheep. I chuckled, as in their lines they looked more like sheep than the animals that were being sold for sacrifice.

The streets were alive with talk about the arrest of the man called Jesus. I knew at once that this Jesus was the leader of the group that had used my room. I knew that it was senseless for me to try to get my money from him. Where would I find him, in a jail? His followers had apparently all fled right after Jesus was arrested in the garden.

I thought that I should at least try to find the one with the purse. I found out that his name was Judas. One temple guard told me that he had done some job for the Sanhedrin and had just been paid handsomely, so I knew that he had money and some of it was due me.

I searched the narrow streets, describing him to people and asking them if they had seen him. One lad pointed in the direction that he had seen Judas rushing. I ran, determined to catch him and collect my money. I found Judas all right. I found him swaying in the breeze with a rope around his neck. I will never forget that sight as long as I live. All this trouble over a fee for a rented room! In my haste to get away from there, I slipped and fell and found myself face to face with more gold coins than I could ever earn in a year. I picked one up. It scalded my hand. The coin must have been in the sun too long. I dropped it and fled to the security of my home. I decided that I would rather face my wife than risk getting involved with anything more concerning this strange group.

On my way, I once again encountered the leader. He was not in a position to pay me either. I found him hanging from a cross for all to see. I froze and allowed panic to creep into me. It was like the feeling when stepping into a winter stream. It jolted through my entire body and paralyzed me in my steps.

One on a cross, another swaying from a tree, and the rest in hiding. Then I noticed the young one, standing there, taller than all of those older than him.

I thought back to that Passover Supper. Jesus spoke of his death and here it was happening. He put himself into the bread and the wine. Remnants of that meal were still sitting on my table. I had become so engrossed in collecting my due that I had neglected to clear away the remains of the meal. Something inside me burned to return and taste the bread and drink the wine.

I realized that this was no ordinary man that had used my room and stirred the anger of the righteous. Perhaps what I had heard was true after all. He is the Promised One. He would die, but I knew he would return. My heart had known he would return when he left my room.

When I left him there that day, I left my cares and concerns about collecting what I thought was due me. I would return to my wife and tell her we were already paid far beyond what money could buy.

Jairus' Daughter

But he took her by the hand and
called out, "Child, get up!"
Her spirit returned, and
she got up at once.

Luke 8:54–55

Jairus' Daughter

The wisdom of youth is constantly overlooked. They say we are too young and have not lived long enough to understand life's trials and tribulations, joys and sorrows. I discovered very quickly that my voice, though quite different from many of the voices that fill our days and our world, is never taken seriously. So I speak little and look much. And I see people so engrossed in the petty and unimportant issues of life that they miss the joy of each day. I see people putting effort into things that really matter little. And these are called the wise ones! I have come to understand that, in this young body of mine, I possess a greater vision than most who are blessed by a greater number of years. He gave me this gift.

You see, I was cold and dead and was warmed back to another chance at living. I was gone although I had never really left. I was about to go home to my Creator, but was called to remain.

The day of my rebirth is one I will remember as long as I have breath in my body. I will relive the feelings I experienced that day with every day I live.

I knew I was dying. I felt the cold creeping gently into my feet and spreading its tendrils until they enclosed my heart. A fear, unlike any I had ever known, entered my mind as the feeling moved slowly and purposefully upward. When the coldness reached my heart, the fear left me and was replaced by an inner peace such as I had never known. The last thing I remember is the din and wailing of those keeping vigil in the house. I longed to reach out and comfort them and put an end to their mourning. I wanted them to realize that my morning was just dawning!

The sound of the inconsolable wailing faded and was replaced with a sweet inner music. I was drawn, like a moth to the light, to the Source of love that created each of us. I felt free and found. I felt young and old. I felt new and yet a part of everything that ever was. I felt the worries and fears of my short years falling off of me like scales off a fish.

Then my journey stopped. Gently I was being beckoned back. My small, cold hands were being warmed. Large, loving hands were encompassing mine and conquering cold, human death, infusing me with new life. I felt as if I was leaving the womb once again. I didn't question nor did I fight. I accepted what had to be.

I blinked and saw a face that would have been unremarkable in any crowd of people. But I saw that the face was surrounded with the same light that I had been journeying toward. He called to me gently, "Little girl, get up." With that simple statement I knew that I had to do as he bid.

I smiled and he returned my smile. I never wanted to let go of his hand but I somehow knew that I would feel it again. I knew I had to "get up" and, with my returned life, show others what living was really for. Mine was not a mission to be accomplished in preaching temple wisdom. It was to be a mission of light and warmth, a message of how we choose to live and choose to be with our entire essence. But how would I ever explain to those who had given me human life what I had experienced and what I learned? How could I tell my parents and all the others?

I was greeted with the same wailing that I had heard in my last moments on this earth. Then came a stone silence so tangible that it could be cut with a knife. All eyes were on me when they should have been on him. They were caught up in the miracle of my returned life and missed the significance of the miracle worker. It was then I realized that most people would only see on the basic level of life and miss the gifts all around them.

My parents rushed forward to snatch me from the Lifegiver who had brought me back to them. His first words to my parents were also simple. "Give her something to eat," he said. Before the astonishment had even sunk in, he brought us back to the mundane. He wanted me to be fed!

As he readied to leave, a banquet was prepared and all were invited. Rooted in the earthly, how easily people miss the true gifts of life! At once, the challenge to feed me went astray. The finest of everything was placed before me to feast on. Little did any of them know that I could now feed them with a comfort and promise that could not be found in any food or drink.

Soon those plates were emptied. My parents did their very best to regain life's normal routine. Soon they began to turn away those who had come to gawk at me. Soon they were rationalizing and downplaying what had happened.

But my heart knew my days could never again be the same as before. When we choose to settle for the routine, we are blinded by that which is unimportant. I celebrated life to the fullest. I saw his face in everything. I rejoiced in the sun, reminded of the warmth that will call all of us home. I spent my days noticing things that I had never really looked at before, like the grace with which a butterfly lands on a flower, or the way the earth soaks in water when the heavens open up. "Come out of the rain. You'll catch your death of a cold!" my mother would call. I often smiled at that and thought of how, as we run from the rain seeking shelter, we miss how Yahweh takes care of everything, even those things we take for granted. And even my grandmother's lecturing—"Learn how to cook!"—made me question how food, which fills a temporary need, would ever be enough for me. A unique rock, a piece of broken and discarded pottery, a trip to the well, all had a different meaning for me after seeing life from the other side. Each day brought innumerable chances to see beyond the ordinariness of life. But no one will ever understand that unless they really open their eyes and their hearts.

The world turned and days went by. I learned to exist on one level and find shelter in another. How I longed to see him who had grasped my hand and changed my heart! Then one day his face flashed in front of me. But this time his face was changing and twisting. I was hit with a blast of frigid air and the coldness started again in my feet. I didn't fear that I was dying again, but I knew that he was about to return home and that I needed to be there for him who had called me back. I flew from my house. My parents called after me, but I ran, not thinking about what direction to take. I just knew that I would find him.

A storm was approaching. The air was changing and many on the roads were becoming fearful. But I knew that I was getting close to the core of my life's destination. The rain came and people scattered like ants returning to their underground hills. I kept going, wanting to be there for him. The earth shook and many grabbed trees and walls, looking for support. I kept going, knowing there was nothing to cling to that could bring me comfort and safety except his hand.

I was about to enter the city, when I heard a familiar sound— a sound that brought the chill closer to my heart—mourning and wailing. I stopped. I knew I would find him right beyond those sounds of terror.

It was then that I saw him. He was in a woman's arms, lying on the ground there in the rain. As I approached, the wailing assailed my ears. When I saw his face, I realized that this stage of his life was over.

I grasped his hand to beckon him back but found it cold and broken. At the touch, I was filled with fear, fear that all that I had felt had only been a dream. My mind was racing. Was it all the delusions of a sick child? Was it a false vision that I had been following since that day? Was I the fool who had chosen the wrong course of life? Had all I had felt been nothing but foolishness?

They began to move him to a tomb carved in the rock. I reached down to help, but since I was small, I was pushed aside. And, being a good little girl, I quickly accepted that role. It was then that it happened. Somehow I knew at that moment that I had indeed chosen the right course. Something shifted inside and I knew what I experienced was real. It was not a dream, nor were my days spent for naught. I knew my decision to gather light and life was the right one. I knew that to be truly fed, we had to let go of roles and expectations and allow life to unfold before our eyes.

Determinedly, I pushed past those people who wanted to keep me a "little girl," and I grasped his feet. When I touched them, there was still a little warmth left in them—enough to banish the last remnants of cold doubt within me.

I helped carry him to the hewn-out rock. As we placed him gently in the tomb, I heard the echoes of human wailing and sorrow bouncing off the cold hard surfaces of this small place. He laid in his temporary bed, like a caterpillar enclosed for only a short time in a cocoon. As I was about to let go of his warm, grace-filled feet, I silently whispered one simple request that I knew would be fulfilled. I leaned down, kissed those broken human feet that had brought others back to the larger road of life, and said to him, "Remember...get up!"

Martha

But the Lord answered her;
"Martha, Martha, you are worried
and distracted by many things;
there is need of only one thing...."

Luke 10:41–42

Martha

My life was always so normal, so routine, so pleasing to everyone—everyone except myself. Then Jesus entered our lives.

I had always done what was needed. I was always the proper one, the right one, the dutiful one. I knew what was expected of me and exceeded expectations. The world around me was alive while my world was routine. Colors flashed from dawn to dusk while I lived in a beige world of normalcy.

The death of my brother taught me that there was no sin in dying, only in not living. I was alive, but I had never lived. I functioned, but I never felt. I performed, but for the wrong audience.

All of that began to change the day Jesus came into our home and our lives. He walked in quite casually and when he left, nothing was quite the same ever again.

We strive to keep everything balanced. Sometimes in this striving to maintain a peaceful existence, we can lose everything we are. Churned soil mixes the proper elements to produce new life. A storm-tossed sea uncovers treasures that have been buried for centuries. But a straight path, travelled unswervingly and routinely, has no room for unexpected wild flowers.

I tried to make everyone as normal as me. My world was tidy and neat, organized and lifeless. I worked at being staid for fear of truly living. But the world crumbles slowly around you when you do not recognize yourself. How strange it was the morning after he was raised to see Lazarus sitting at the breakfast table.

But I am ahead of myself. The influence of Jesus in my life began when I wanted him to influence my sister Mary to be more like me. Mary never settled into routine. She was a good woman but I thought she needed to learn to discipline herself. We did not have the same views about what was important. Mary never seemed to accept a woman's role. I thought Jesus could show her the error of her ways.

Jesus's reaction was not one I expected. At first I was furious, not at his siding with Mary, but at his challenging me to be someone I really wanted to be but had denied for years. Very gently he churned my inner seas and tossed about a lifetime of my working purposefully at being routine. People always say that others stop our inner growth. The truth is that we stop our own growth and settle into complacency. A life truly lived is never tidy and neat. We choose our own destiny.

When Jesus departed from our home, after gently wiping the dust from the hidden treasure within me, I was left with a fascinating stranger—me. I sat long that night, finally watching the dark fade into crimson dawn. The first light of dawn blessed me with a new sense of vision. For many days that seemed endlessly new, I saw familiar things with a different eye. I experienced a new self, existing in a new world. The old didn't pass away; it just was not as important. I was still myself, but I was giving myself more liberties, more permissions, more life! I relished the chance to forgive myself the sin of never living.

Then Lazarus died. My life stopped. I fell right back into the tasks of the routine. I made sure that all of the funeral guests were comfortable, the house clean, the meals cooked, to the point of sacrificing my own feeling in the doing. I longed to see Jesus. I needed to share my grief. I needed the reassurance to allow my new self to resurface, but Jesus was nowhere to be found. Word finally came to us that he was on his way. Why was his way not my way? I needed him to be here, but I was left alone. Cold fear of returning to my former ways began to grip me as strongly as the coldness of death that enveloped my brother.

I felt his presence before he entered our home. I threw caution to the wind and ran to meet him. I needed him so! When I saw him, I realized that he had never left. That day he raised Lazarus, I realized that he was permanently in me, perpetually giving me permission. He returned my self to me.

As I stand by his cross on this day, shaken by his agony and approaching death, there are things I know with a surety that keeps me whole. I know the life he gave me and will forever give me. He will die, but I know he will never be dead. As much as I thought I needed his permission to live, I know I must give him permission to die in order to stay alive.

His life was never routine. Neither is his death. There is no sin in dying. There is sin in never being alive. Forever, he will live in me and in all others who seek permission to deny daily death and cling to the victory of life.

A Roman Centurion

And to the centurion Jesus said;
"Go; let it be done for you
according to your faith."

Matthew 8:13

A Roman Centurion

I am a controlled man. I have learned to feel in private and be decisive in public. I have never wavered nor questioned my superiors. My world is one of obeying orders and issuing orders. It is a system that works well for me and I for it.

Today I find myself pacing my rooms, and shaking my head. I have ordered my soldiers to guard crucifixions more times than the number of years that I have been on this earth. But to order my men to guard this man Jesus as he is crucified today, wrenched my heart.

I had met Jesus only once and found him to be a good man. I had gone to him to ask for his help in restoring health to one of my favorite servants. Good servants are so hard to come by and a loyal one is a rarity that should be nurtured. When mine became deathly ill, I sought out the finest doctors. Their diagnoses were all the same...inevitable death. I was frantic, not only because I was losing a good servant, but also because I had come to love and respect this man, although I have never said this out loud to any human being.

I had heard that this Jesus was a healer. There are so many magicians and healers in this strange land that I thought it could do no harm. So I walked with a cohort to find him and see if he could help. I never imagined that in asking that my servant be healed that I, myself, would be thrust into such turmoil.

Walking with Jesus

I gave this Jesus the proper amount of respect as I asked him for his help. And then it happened. This Jesus looked into my eyes and knew who I was. I saw in him a leader far greater than any I had ever served under. I looked at his followers and saw a loyalty that stemmed from love rather than discipline. I saw the faces of the people who were following him, people who were joyful at being near him. I saw in him just how empty my life had become.

I realized he was more than just another man for in those brief moments, he freed my heart. Jesus looked at me and I was bathed in his love and warmth. People like me do not feel love, let alone express it publicly. Yet, there I was, in front of men under my command, professing a faith in this Jesus that I didn't even know I had. The truths we utter when we do not think too carefully about what we are saying are astounding!

As soon as I finished declaring what I knew Jesus could do, I started to regret that my words were spoken in such a public forum. But the problem with words is that no matter what we say or do, we can never call them back. I hoped that no one had heard what I said. But that was not to be. Jesus repeated my words for all to hear and called what I had, "faith." Until now, "faith" had always meant knowing what I had to do, and when and how to get it done quickly and efficiently.

When I returned home, I found that my servant got better the moment that Jesus said he was healed. My servant was fine, but I was anything but fine! Jesus had gone his way and I had gone mine, but I could not escape his grasp on my heart.

As the days past, my servant became a constant reminder of my meeting with Jesus. This man, whom I reached out to help, now became a living, breathing reminder to me of the void in my life. He began to give me looks that said he knew what turmoil I was living in. I put distance between the two of us. I barked a few orders at him just to maintain that distance, but he didn't even flinch. He just kept looking at me as if he could see right through

70

me. How could this man, to whom I had only given orders, ever comprehend who I am or the confusion inside of me?

My career in the military began to slip. I started listening to the needs of my men rather than being assertive. I started to feel things around me and even question some of the things my superiors ordered me do. I lived with the realization that I had never met anyone more superior than this man Jesus. On a dusty road, in this Godforsaken country, on a journey of desperation, I had met a man who changed my life!

I decided I must see Jesus again. But, as things turned out, that was not to be. I had told my men to keep me informed of anything they heard about this man. I let them think they were serving the Roman government when, in actuality, they were serving my inner needs.

The events that led to this dreadful day happened so fast. Last night, as I was giving a banquet which I hoped would help re-establish my status in the military, I was given a message. Just as my servant was placing a dish in front of me, one of my soldiers told me Jesus and his followers had celebrated the Passover and how at the meal Jesus told his men that he no longer called them "servants." Rather he called them "friends" because "they knew what their master was all about." He also told me that Jesus was arrested and taken to Pilate for questioning. The food that was being served froze in mid-air as my servant's eyes locked into mine. That smile again returned to his face as small drops of sweat formed above my lip.

This morning I was ordered to dispatch a guard to keep order at the crucifixions of three men. I didn't give it a second thought, until I learned that one of the three men was Jesus. The Jews wanted Jesus killed, but they wanted Rome to do it.

Although I usually lead my guard to their assignment, this day I could not. I stayed in my home, feigning illness in order not to be at the cross. I didn't realize just how true my excuse was until I gave into my heart-sickness. Now I pace and I wait.

The skies are becoming so dark.

The winds are beginning to whip and there is moisture in the air. This barren land is about to receive an unusual storm. Maybe it will water some new life into this vast sand dune of a country! I welcome the dark clouds for they match my mood as I retreat inside to the security of my home and my self.

What harm did this Jesus do to be given such a sentence? I will never understand these people who profess to be guided by religion and yet treat their own in such an ungodly manner. What cruelty exists in their hearts to have turned such venom on this good man? All I know is that Jesus healed my servant without touching him, or even seeing him. That power still has me most disturbed. And there were his eyes...cutting surer than a surgeon's knife to expose the very core of my being. They reached inside of me and touched a secret place that I had kept hidden so well that even I had forgotten its existence.

Suddenly a shudder runs through me. I know in my heart that Jesus has died. I don't know how I know it, but I am sure that he has died.

My insides are in turmoil. My throat becomes parched and I call to my servant to bring me some wine to remove the dryness that seems like it will be caught there forever.

The winds whip and the trees bow. The earth shakes and my heart pounds. I know one other thing. The memory of this Jesus will never leave me. How can this be? We Romans have an answer for everything in life and this just doesn't seem logical. I see my entire life flash before me as if the moments of goodness and evil are being weighed.

I tremble because I know that I have come face to face with my true superior. What can this mean for the rest of my life? What will I do? I have lost my effectiveness as an officer. I struggle to maintain my balance but I know I have lost my detachment. If I return to Rome, I will be disgraced and ridiculed. I know that I am different and, in that difference, can no longer conceive a course for my life.

My servant brings me wine but my hands are shaking too much to pick up the goblet. It is then that a soldier comes bursting into the room. He is babbling about the death of Jesus. Whispering, as a child seeking parental wisdom, I ask if Jesus said anything before he died. My soldier looks at me and thinks. I hold my wine in a hand struggling to be still, and start to bring it to my lips. But before I can taste the quenching liquid, he remembers something that Jesus said, "Forgive them, for they know not what they do."

The goblet slips from my fingers and falls to the ground. I don't hear the sound of the cup hitting the floor as the crash in my brain overwhelms me. My soldier backs out of the room, afraid of what he sees happening to me.

My servant calmly picks up the goblet, replaces the spilled wine with water and holds it to my lips. I drink as if too feeble to care for myself. I meet my servant's eyes finally, and realizing that Jesus lives within my heart, I am suddenly no longer afraid. In a very small voice, stripped of all pretense, I say very quietly... "Thank you, my friend."

Mary Magdalene

And a woman in the city, who was a sinner, having learned that [Jesus] was eating in the Pharisee's house, brought an alabaster jar of ointment.

Luke 7:37

Mary Magdalene

As I stand here at his cross, I long to tell him of the influence he has had on my life, an influence that will change the course of it for the rest of my days. My heart tells me that he knows, though. I hold up his grief-filled mother, supported by love for him who gave me new life and taught me to stand free.

For too long I struggled with the exhausting battle of living two lives. Everyone knew me as the town harlot, loud and garish, loose and tawdry. No one knew the gentle woman enclosed within. No one, until Jesus came along.

It is so hard to live a dual existence. Daily survival becomes an ongoing battle. I spent most of my time and energy keeping alive the inner person that only I knew was there. People made it difficult for me to be what my heart knows I am. People might have disapproved of who I was, but they always wanted a part in shaping that person. If only people turned some of their energy inward instead of wasting it telling others who they should be, this world would never have put Jesus on the cross.

The townspeople jeered and taunted me the prostitute, but never gave me a chance to be anything else. I suppose most people need someone to taunt—some to divert attention from their own faults, others to feel powerful, and still others just because they fear standing in opposition to the crowd. Few people allow others to be the people they want to be. It is the rare person who pushes back another's inner curtain shielding private possibilities and allows the real you to shine through. For me, that person was Jesus!

The first time that he touched my hand I felt an internal jolt. I had been touched so often to satisfy the needs of others that I had felt calloused, both inside and out. I had become more than a prostitute—I had become a hard and unfeeling woman. It was the only way I could keep alive that small spark of life flickering within me. For me, turning my back on life was the only way to survive—until I met him.

No one ever considered that I could have needs. Rather, I was used for the needs of others. Men used my body for their needs, and when their physical desires were satisfied, they would abuse me verbally to satisfy their inner needs. I don't know what repulsed me more, the calloused hands that groped at my body, or the calloused words that tore at my heart. Fathers used to shield their children from my path in the light of day and then make their way to my bed at night. I don't know what they needed more, a town prostitute or a town scapegoat.

The more people would taunt me, the more I would flaunt my role. We are all actors on the stage of life, after all! But then, at the end of each day's performance, the curtain comes down and the audience goes home. Then who are we left with, the actor or the real person? It is too easy to continue the acting and deny the reality.

I played the harlot very well. I walked boldly to the market and glared at those who snickered and whispered about me.

I was never able to figure out why people whispered. What good words ever needed to be uttered in hushed tones? I pretended not to hear the hurtful words others spoke. I often wondered why, if people had something bad to say about you, they always made sure that they said it so you could hear. The more evil and hurtful the taunts, the more publicly they were spoken!

Mary Magdalene

I never concealed the fact that I was the town prostitute. My dress spoke of it, my manner proclaimed it, and the stream of men at my door confirmed it.

I blamed all of my problems on others. Cynicism and bitterness became powerful partners in my life. People blamed me for everything that was wrong in the town and I, in turn, blamed them for my problems. That solution works until you are alone with yourself. Then reality sets in. We spend the majority of our lives with ourselves, but love ourselves the least. We breathe every moment of our lives in order to live, but we rarely breathe in what we truly need to live! From dawn to last light, we think but we rarely give any thought to what would make us truly happy.

Every night, when my house was finally empty, I would place the gold coins in a small box on my table and attempt to open the inner box of self to find some glittering gold within. That task was becoming more and more difficult—until Jesus entered my life.

I went to him in the light of day. I pushed others aside in order for him to look at me. I didn't realize until our eyes met that I went to him, not as the prostitute, but as a child of need—vulnerable and yet hopeful. I needed him to touch a part of me that had never been touched—my heart.

I had not cried since childhood. I needed to keep my tears inside to water the oasis that existed in the midst of the self-imposed desert of my personhood. When his eyes met mine, he saw my needs, and years of stored tears were released.

When I was in his presence, I no longer had to play a part. I could be who I knew I always was. People have spent endless hours arguing about who Jesus was. I never argue. I know he made me realize who I am. The saddest thing that can happen is for a person to settle on a life of living lies. When we live such a life, we bend the tender tree within ourselves to the winds of others' whims. The tree is misshapen by those winds and we are doomed to live a life of lies. Few people love us for who we are. Most people love us for what they need from us. All too often we settle on this "love" that never gives us anything.

The gaze of Jesus stopped the winds of others from bending that tender tree within me. The love in his eyes looked beyond the prostitute and sought out the real me.

The tears came in the haven of Jesus's loving eyes. My neediness would no longer hold me a tortured captive. I would not be alone again, nor would I play a part alien to my true inner self. Jesus became my strength. I could openly proclaim the me I had kept in the recesses of my heart. There was no need to worry about the words of others, words meant to hurt me. I could be the true me, not just for an agonizing, solitary moment, but for the rest of my life.

I cried for a long time. My tears washed his sacred feet that led me down the path of wholeness. Until that moment, I always believed that crying showed weakness and gave others power over me. But now I unabashedly gave my power to Jesus, knowing that his power would fill this hollow, aching vessel.

When the tears stopped and he took my hand, my inner desert flowered. His spirit uncovered future possibilities that I never knew existed. He drew the final curtain on the part I had played. He peeled away so many layers of pain that I had denied for so long. He made it no longer necessary to conceal my true self behind curtains of lies.

With his touch came the endless dawns of new days. With his touch came an unfolding of possibilities that I had never dared imagine. Into my barrenness came gardens of glory. With his touch, his spirit entered my soul. His spirit gave me the courage to stop acting. His spirit moved me gently and changed me radically. His spirit blocked out the whispers of others who never again would tell me how to live or who to be. His spirit joined mine and gave me life.

Now his life is draining away and the whispers of others are swirling like the scorching desert wind. "Save yourself...Come down from that cross..." I wanted to scream, "Why? To enter your sphere and be forever captive to your whims and needs?" The whispers pummel me from all sides like physical blows, even more hurtful because I love him so.

He is dying and I am still living! How I wish I could change places with him!

His words cut through the whispers of recrimination and the wails of our sorrow. He calls for his mother and I hesitantly release her into the arms of the young man named John. I stand alone, left to remember the day his spirit filled me with new meaning.

He is becoming weaker. I feel his life seeping away, though I struggle to keep that spirit alive within me. Thunder roars from the sky, drowning out the whispers below.

He lifts his head one final time and for just a moment looks at me again. I hold my breath. His eyes pierce my soul and I hear him say, "Into your hands I commend my spirit." With that he is gone.

I feel the blood that courses through my veins, and know, with clarity, that it is his life that surges through my body. His spirit lives on.

The Paralyzed Man Made Whole

When Jesus saw their faith, he said to the paralytic man, "Son, your sins are forgiven."

Mark 2:5

The Paralyzed Man Made Whole

I had to come today. My legs and my feet drew me here. As I see the agony of him who made my journey possible, my mind wanders backward in time...

I shall never forget the humiliation of relying on others for mobility. I remember the agony and the struggle of having a man's mind in a useless body. I don't know what ached more, the pain of being paralyzed, or the humiliation of needing help to do the simple things that others take so for granted.

I dared not hope that this Jesus would change my life that day when I was lowered through that roof. I can remember the racing of my heart as my friends let me down into the room. I cringed at the thought of so unusual an entrance, but, when I caught a glimpse of the holy man, nothing else mattered.

I knew right away that I was face to face with someone who did not pity me. Here was someone who did not turn his gaze uncomfortably away but rather looked right into my soul. His eyes affirmed me and proclaimed, in deafening silence, that I was a whole person in spite of my deformed body.

When he demanded that I stand up and walk, terror grabbed at my heart. Walk? Never! But a wellspring of courage was prying apart the icy fingers that were clutching my heart. At his command, I took the first step that would redirect the journey of my life, because he believed in me.

His challenge to "go home" confused me. My heart told me that I was home. The safety and security of "home" for me was now solidly rooted in his life and his message. But freedom was suddenly mine! My legs, which had never walked before, would take me to places that my mind's eye had only seen in dreams. My hands, once bent and gnarled, could now reach out to others who were neglected and overlooked.

But as I stand here at his cross, I wonder how this could have happened to one who did so much good. Slowly I step closer to him. It is all so wrong. It is all so ironic. He hangs in the center of two others. He, the center of our lives and our universe, he who brought wholeness to others, is now broken and shattered.

I, who had been so used to others staring at me, hope now that his gaze would not come my way. As if reading my thoughts, he turns his tortured head and looks me in the eye. Gathering what seems to be super-human strength, he makes one request—"I thirst."

My legs feel paralyzed once again. I stand here unable to move, frozen in my helplessness in the face of the excruciating pain suffered by him who was the source of my healing.

How I want to fulfill his needs as he had filled my life's needs! But I am unable to move!

I feel old feelings coursing through my body and realize that, though my body is whole, my spirit is not. As if carefully orchestrated by the powers of darkness, I feel my legs becoming as they had once been. Again I begin to feel vulnerable and dependent upon others for my life's sustenance.

Things begin to happen very quickly. Soldiers who mocked his every word take a sponge and dip it in vinegar and wine and put it to his lips.

In a brief moment that will haunt me my whole life, his eyes once again catch mine and ignite my soul. With blood staining his face and gall dripping through his beard, he looks right at me. In that one moment trapped in time, he silently reassures me with one unspoken word that I can hear clearly in the depths of my being — "courage."

I know immediately that the fire he had started in my life could never be extinguished. I know that never again would darkness cover me now that I stand in his light. I realize that true healing and wholeness are journeys of a lifetime and the only roadblocks we meet are the self-imposed ones of wanting others to accept us and fearing that they won't.

I realize that on the day when I was lowered through the roof, I had been given only the seed of courage and that it would grow only if I allowed it to.

I start moving once again. I had been momentarily paralyzed by fear, the strongest force for stopping the forward progress of life. Now I walk again—but differently. I pace my steps, which do not draw me closer to his cross but away from it.

I know why I was drawn to this place. I understand that even though my limbs could move, my being had been thirsting. Now my inner thirst of trying to be like others had finally been quenched. In this place, he would, once and forever, end people's thirsting.

I leave the cross, turning away to seek another home, this time in the life's journeys of those who find themselves paralyzed with fear.

I look up at a darkening sky and see the roof over him being opened. His Father is calling him home. I glance back at him. His head is bowed, his body lifeless. I speak from my heart as I return to him one final sentiment….Courage…courage, my friend, my Lord.

One of the Three Magi

*...[the wise men] set out, and there,
ahead of them, went the star that they
had seen at its rising, until it stopped
over the place where the child was.*

Matthew 2:9

One of the Three Magi

All of the world loves to watch a juggler. Even adults, as they contentedly watch their children entranced by a performer, are, in reality, themselves fascinated by the juggler. Children watch a juggler, amazed at what he can do. Adults watch a juggler, often waiting for him to drop a ball. And if he does drop one, all the skill he previously exhibited is forgotten. How often I have seen adults try to distract a juggler, hoping he would drop a ball, and then, they, the cause of the distraction, walk away, shaking their heads and bemoaning his lack of talent.

I have always been fascinated by jugglers. Many have performed for me, tossing up balls, knives, fire, and all sorts of other things. During the performance, I never really look at the juggler, but like everyone else, watch what he is doing, never seeing the person. When it is over, I spend time talking with the juggler. While my conversations with these traveling entertainers haven't taught me the art of juggling, they have made me realize that most of us are jugglers in life

Think about it. A juggler needs to watch over each item that he is juggling, giving each one the correct amount of time and balance. When things work well, the juggler can keep everything in its proper place and all of the items dance through the air at the juggler's seemingly effortless command. Don't you see? We all juggle things in life. We spend all of our time juggling people, roles, jobs, tasks, ideas, dreams and even our own needs. Where we fail as jugglers is that our own needs are often the last things we put into motion and the first things that we drop.

Jesus was crucified for being a false prophet, but he was a master juggler. Few people will ever see this and will think this is a laughable statement. But then, I have been told that I look at life differently than most people. It was that different perspective that made me journey to that manger so long ago.

My journey began when I saw that the skies were being juggled to proclaim his birth. It is a sad fact of life that although we are blessed with the gift of sight every waking moment of our lives, we rarely look at things. If more people took the time to look at things and see how our entire universe is balanced together into a masterful mosaic, the loving hand of our Creator would be constantly obvious.

I was amazed that so few took notice of the brilliant star proclaiming a monumental event. I truly expected that the roads would be jammed with people following the star, but there were just the three of us and a few shepherds. I am sure that many saw the star and its beckoning light, but few were willing to toss their lives into the air and risk a journey whose destination they did not know in advance. Life is like that. We really have no control over what happens to us, but we do maintain complete control over how we react to what life juggles to us.

I have been accused of thinking too much. Thinking is a nonstop curse but a daily blessing. To think enables us to grow. To think enables us to juggle the complacency of life that feels like a friendly blanket, a deceptively comfortable blanket that can doom us to a life with no risks. Just as people become quickly bored with a juggler whose act is routine and lacks excitement, so too will our lives become routine if we settle for juggling life without taking any risks. It is unfortunate that fear keeps most people from juggling risks into their own lives, and they therefore settle on a life of boredom and routine.

And so it was that Jesus was a master juggler. He juggled feelings that people had accepted and were comfortable with. Those who were bitter and angry, dead and sick were juggled into healthy people full of life. In the juggling of Jesus, the individual was tossed into the air, changed, and offered a path out of the routine. Jesus tossed into the air what we thought was impossible and showed us the possibility of it all. The beginning of the possibility was marked by a star. Who could have imagined that a star would move to mark his birth? Who would have thought that death could lose its finality and he would embrace his friend Lazarus again? And who would have thought that bread would become his body? Who would have thought that so many would miss the message of the Word Made Flesh?

Oftentimes, jugglers draw people into their acts. They call for volunteers and no one steps forward, even though, with hearts beating faster, each is hoping to be chosen. Jesus gave everyone the opportunity to be chosen. He spent all of his time juggling hearts and lives, visions and dreams. People always giggle gleefully when the entertainer pulls them in his act. When the demonstration is over, they go home to their comfortable routines and the memory quickly fades. But what Jesus offered when he drew people into his juggling was a chance for life to be changed forever and a memory that would never fade. Some crowds became difficult people to serve. Everyone wants to be entertained. No one wants to be changed.

Most just wanted to watch, sure he would drop what he juggled, angry when he didn't.

Although I have not seen Jesus since our meeting at the manger, I have kept myself informed of his progress. I listened with a mixture of fascination and sadness as I heard of person after person challenging Jesus to fail at his juggling act. The better a juggler is, the more eager the crowds are to see him fail. The better the juggler, the louder his detractors silently watch and wait and hope for his failure. And if that failure doesn't come, the detractors will leave and fabricate stories about the failure of the masterful juggler.

As a person of control, I know we have no control over life. The more frantically we juggle things in our lives, the more we become weary and tired with life itself. It is only when we have the courage to drop what we are juggling that we realize the true message of life. How often do we allow others to influence our lives and make us juggle the gift of ourselves for no other reason than to please someone else? How often do we fall into the trap of letting our detractors make us juggle faster and faster and faster? All of this is a waste of the precious energy we are given for only a while. There has to come a time when we drop our juggling and say "enough!"

When I juggled my life to follow that star, I risked power and prestige and braved the taunts of others to seek the One who would juggle my life. I had no idea where our journey would end.

We brought three gifts with us to this newborn king. Little did we realize then that each of us had chosen a gift symbolic of a great fear that each of us had juggled unsuccessfully in our lives.

One of my companions feared the wealth in his life, that the power behind the gold would change him into a unfeeling person whose major concerns would be centered on wealth. He left gold for Jesus to juggle.

My other companion had a problem communicating with the Creator through prayer. He gave frankincense for Jesus to use as a prayer offering. My friend began praying as soon as he left the juggling to the Christ.

I revel in living and have always feared death. I left myrrh, the ointment of anointing, without ever realizing that I had left my greatest fear in that stable. Jesus, the master juggler, juggled people's lives without most even being aware of it. I have come to understand that the main reason that the Creator gave us a portion of himself was to encourage and challenge us to leave what we endlessly juggle in life to someone else. That someone is Jesus.

My mind knew, as I knelt at the manger, that a baby could not recognize me. But Jesus juggled my heart so much that before I left that stable, I was aware of who I was and what I most needed. I saw that, even then, the Creator was juggling lives and now know he continued to do so with the simple things, such as bread, stars, water, and even wood.

In following Jesus I found that he, too, in his humanity, had to drop what he was juggling and allow his life to be guided by the One who made us all. Slowly, but with all of the purpose in the universe, Jesus stopped pleasing the crowds. He moved from being one who only entertained to one who challenged. People who wanted to be entertained quickly became tired of being challenged to be more. They wanted Jesus to be the one to do more.

His crowd of detractors increased as they watched Jesus, becoming more and more eager for him to fail. He was constantly being tossed more and more items to juggle. He continually took upon himself more and more needs. And, sadly enough, he failed in the eyes of the people who did not want to change.

I realize that he even had to stop juggling the gifts we gave him at the manger in his own life and hand them over to the Creator whom he challenged us to call "Father." He stopped juggling my friend's fear of wealth and power when he was betrayed by a friend for man's money. He stopped juggling my friend's frankincense when he stopped trying to please the temple officials. And finally he dropped my myrrh when he died on the cross. I know that the detractors of Jesus saw this as a victory. The more he suffered, the happier they were. They saw death as an end to this man's juggling of hearts.

When I received the messenger who told me that Jesus had died, I knew that the love of this manger-child would somehow be juggled into a new beginning. Death will be juggled into new life. Hate will be juggled into hope. Fear will be juggled into trust. Pride will be juggled into humility. Detractors' triumph will be juggled into the apparent victim's victory.

My messenger also informed me that when Jesus died, the sky turned black, lightning flashed ripping apart the black clouds, heavy rain fell, and the earth quaked.

Does it surprise me that the sky was juggled to give a message? I think not, for I once followed a juggled sky to find the Master Juggler.

A Temple Official

*Then the chief priests of the Jews said to
Pilate, "Do not write, 'The King of
the Jews,' but, 'This man said,
I am King of the Jews.'"*

John 19:21

A Temple Official

People are like sheep who need to be kept mindless and in line. We do not need anyone to encourage them to think or feel or change. This carpenter's son meant trouble, encouraging people to be themselves. This new world he preaches threatens those at the top. We have plotted too long to allow some unknown to urge people to listen to their hearts rather than listen to us.

I have worked hard to get where I am today. I relish the respect born of fear that I have built up. Fear has no parents for it is conceived free of love. I know what to say and when to say it. I know whom I should speak to and whom I should avoid. I know the right look to make people wither like freshly cut grass in the afternoon sun. People have to be told about the oasis but kept in the desert. What need would there be for us if we led people to water?

There were some in our midst who were swayed by his words. His deeds made us privately tremble as the people we kept downtrodden began to raise their eyes and change their lives.

We killed him, finally. It was like swatting a pesky bug. We did not cause his death. We made sure that we would be blameless when the event took place. But then, it is so easy to get people to turn against the innocent because ordinary people fear power used against them.

It is so easy to sacrifice a person who uses words such as love and forgiveness, for people really want to be told what to do.

There is too much challenge in asking people to feel and love, care and hope. People respond well to rules, not challenges.

I have heard some of the tales of this false messiah. He made so many mistakes, mistakes that made him vulnerable. He made his first major blunder when he placed his trust in people, the wrong people. What good are the poor and the hungry, the prostitutes and the rabble? Deal with the powerful, not the powerless. Move only in acceptable circles.

He should have stayed in one town or one community for an extended period of time to allow his power base to grow. This was another big mistake. This false prophet did too much moving around to firmly establish himself.

And one must claim control. Once you have it, keep it by giving people rules and regulations, not thoughts and visions.

He shouldn't have bothered with parables. People didn't need to hear about birds or flowers or mustard seeds. They need hard, fast rules so they know what is expected.

It was so easy to stir things up by planting rumors about this man. We even found out that people gossiped about his mother before she was married. We were planning to use that dirt, but we never had to. We never needed it. His words alone were enough to nail him to the tree. But those words will soon fade away and be forgotten now that he is gone.

In fact everything went our way until that fox, Pilate, instructed the soldiers to place that sign on his cross. I am sure that my superiors will be furious when they hear that he was titled "King of the Jews." I did my best to have that sign removed, but to no avail.

I can't get upset about it. We got what we wanted: the Nazarene was crucified. Not many people will see the sign. And no one will believe it anyway.

The Thief's Sister

And with him they
crucified two bandits,
one on his right
and one on his left.

Mark 15:27

The Thief's Sister

>>>>+<<<<

I always feared that my brother would go wrong. And now this is how he ends up—hanging there on a cross, with two others, for all of the world to see. I burn with shame as people leaving the city gawk at my brother.

His charges are clearly posted over his head. Although I know he is guilty, the blood that binds me to him makes me long to help him somehow. I watched him grow and tried to be a good influence on him, but he always wanted everything the quick and easy way. The short easy route in life was the one he always chose. My brother never owned up to anything. He always felt that life had overlooked him and had given him a bad deal. Everything bad in life was someone else's fault. Even now he is still stubbornly trying to hide his pain, but I can see it—his pain and his humiliation. There he is, crucified for all to see, and still attempting to hold his head high in defiance.

His friend has been crucified with him. Strange that they would put the two of them on either side of this one who claimed to be the Messiah. They form a strange trinity of pain and condemnation.

There is so much clamoring from people jeering at this Jesus. I heard him preach a few times. He said such wonderful things! He talked of taking care of those in need and loving your neighbor. His words touched me deeply and made me stop and look at my life. But then, look where that kind of weird talk got him! He is right there with my brother who only used words for his own gain and never gave any thought to the consequences of his words.

Perhaps a bit of my brother's cynicism lives within me too. People seem to live only for themselves. No one is willing to help those in need. No one stands by another when the crowds turn against that person. Even the followers of this Jesus have abandoned him and are hiding in the protective hills.

There are just a few women near him now. Someone said that one is his mother. No one notices me, though I, too, share in the grief of this day. I need to be near my brother in this, his hour of need. With a boldness I am not certain I really feel, I walk closer to his cross.

I look up at my brother. Pain is etched on his face. I tell him that I am here, I am with him. My heart cries out in desolation for the little boy I once held on my lap. I wish he was brave enough to show the whole world the loving, gentle man he truly is. He always wanted desperately to be recognized, to be the center of attention. He thought that by stealing he could gain that recognition. Well, now he is getting plenty of attention, hanging there, naked for all to see, writhing in agony. And now, no one else will ever know the real man inside the thief on the cross.

His friend on the other cross is starting to mock Jesus. I can't believe that a person in such a circumstance could have the audacity to mock another in the same situation. I see my brother struggling to get some air into him so that he too can speak. I want to scream! I can't stand any more of his bravado. If he only knew when to keep his mouth shut, he might have stayed out of trouble! The words come out and much to my surprise, he is chastising the other thief for his cruel words to Jesus. Can it be that my brother is speaking out for the needs of someone else?

My mind is swirling with confusion and the emotion of the day. Maybe I am imposing my hopes into his words. Did my brother just admit to being a thief? I am stunned by the sincerity in his words and the public outpouring of the goodness that my brother kept so well hidden all his life.

My brother's words are now openly proclaiming the innocence of this man Jesus! He is supporting this man in front of everyone. He is doing more than those who followed him for years!

Jesus's mother now turns and looks at me. She knows who I am. The look of love that transcends her sorrow is one that draws me closer to my brother, closer to her, and closer to her son. A circle of pain joins us and I know I am not alone in my mourning.

My brother speaks again, his body tortured with the very effort. I strain to listen, no longer afraid of what will come from his mouth. I know my brother has conquered the darkness within him. Not boldly, not mockingly, but with an urgency and humility of a man filled with love and conviction, he asks Jesus to remember him when he gets to his kingdom. Such a simple request from a man who spent his life seeking the wrong things! In these agonizing moments, my brother finally seeks a recognition that transcends the worldly. The kingdom he seeks now is not one built on gold or silver, but rather on the heavenly.

This Jesus, so frail and looking so small, struggles to turn his bleeding head toward my brother. Will Jesus condemn him for his past sins? Will he chastise him? His mother looks at me as I hold my breath and wait to hear what Jesus has to say. There is no condemnation in his words. Jesus speaks to him with a gentleness, love, and hope unlike I have ever heard before. The words are borne from his heart. My soul rejoices as Jesus promises my brother that he will be with him today in paradise. Those words bring me back to reality. My brother is going to die. He spent his life searching for paradise, usually in the goods of others. Now he has been promised true paradise, one without earthly constraints. The smile that his mother gives me warms away the chill of fearing what the promise of Jesus implies.

Walking with Jesus

I now realize they have crucified the true Messiah. Jesus reached through the darkness that had surrounded my brother and released a light that I always knew was there.

I stand near my brother knowing that, although a thief was crucified, a different man now suffers on that cross. At last someone noticed him, recognized him for the good person that he had hidden inside and accepted him for what he could be. At last, he will find paradise! I feel consolation in my grief and relief in my desolation as I realize that my brother, in his dying moments, has been reborn.

As Jesus dies, the ground shakes. What a powerful acknowledgment of his divinity it is as it seems all of nature is crying for the world's loss. Many who had been blinded to his goodness cower in fear.

I shall not soon forget the agonized screams of my brother as they broke his legs. In the overpowering waves of sorrow that engulf me at my brother's death, I also find an oasis of peace in knowing that he is now with Jesus.

As I wait for them to remove my brother's body from the cross, I find myself walking over to the mother of the dead Jesus. I hesitantly touch her shoulder, wishing I could allay her pain at the death of her son. As she turns to me, I am overwhelmed by her anguish. I want to give her a bit of the strength that she had given me, but I can't find the words. Her eyes tell me none are needed.

As I turn away to take the lifeless body of my brother to his final resting place, I touch his cold and battered face. As I look at him one last time, I am consoled knowing he has found his paradise—a true and lasting one.

Thank God—and thank the One crucified!

A Soldier at the Cross

"Truly this man was God's Son!"

Matthew 27:54

A Soldier at the Cross

Today is a day I want to forget. Usually I am not bothered by taking part in a crucifixion. It is part of my job. And if Rome is to maintain her empire and her superiority, then we have to teach her enemies a lesson. But this man...

This man bothered me from the first. He unsettled something deep inside of me, and I found the granite I had built up within me, through years of conditioning, begin to crumble. He is not like any other man I have ever met and certainly not like any other one in his circumstances. I am to walk with him to his execution place. Two others have already made their way there. It seems a simple assignment, certainly one I have done many times before. But there is something about him that struck me from the first. He has a truly regal bearing. Though his face is streaked with blood and his head is crowned with a symbol of Roman mockery, he is erect and his stance powerful. The look on his face is one of freedom rather than fear or defiance. And in his eyes there is an assurance and peacefulness unlike anything I have ever encountered before. When I first saw him some of my interior beliefs began to tremble. I know we can bury things within ourselves and convince all is for the best. I had always lived that way quite comfortably, but when I saw him, I began to wonder just how comfortable my life had been in all reality.

From the first I had to push myself to carry out my orders and ignore what was happening inside me. As he is about to begin his last journey, he looks at the beam of his cross. There is still no fear in him. He gingerly touches the wood and glances upward. What could he be looking for at a time like this? One of the other guards snatches away the purple robe that covered him and pushes him to begin. I walk in front of him.

The crowds are ugly. These festival days are not the best of days to guard a prisoner on his way to crucifixion. I was sure that Rome was once again going to be the target of their taunts and jeers. How wrong I was! The slurs that were usually directed toward us are being hurled at him instead. I am always amazed at just how vicious people can be when they are bent on destroying another! He is going to die a horrible death! What more did they want from him?

He is a small man, not very muscular. I know that he will have difficulty maneuvering these crooked, winding streets, paved with uneven stones. Imperceptibly, I slow my pace. Why? Why am I feeling anything towards this man?

I have lived a guarded life. Back in Rome I leaned towards a life of letters and words. I loved being in the presence of those wise men who could light fires in my heart or unleash currents of emotions with their inspired words. But my parents had other plans for my life. They convinced me that the best thing for everyone, especially me, was to sign up for military service. The steely glint in my father's eyes and the resigned look on my mother's face told me there was no dissuading them from what they had decided for me.

I endured the first few months of my service, a period dedicated to breaking the individual so that he would serve unquestioningly. I learned that the less you thought, the further you went. I resigned myself quickly to a life of being told what to do, although I wondered for a long time why questioning was so bad. If thinking differently was so wrong, why did we have the capacity to do so?

A Soldier at the Cross

I find the gap between us widening. He is slowing down. No man in his condition could endure this type of journey. I'm not sure which is more draining, the weight of the cross or the constant abuse of the people.

The only true friends that he seems to have are the women. They follow him, weeping and lamenting. They are brave and strong women—women who don't seem to care about the opinion of the crowd. Can I consider myself strong, or am I, in reality, weak? Haven't I caved in to the pressure of people who told me what to do with my life? Why do we listen to others when our heart is beating in a different direction? These women are calling out to him..."Son of God"..."Messiah"..."Anointed One." The gender of the heart is professing belief while the gender of power is cursing him. I had never encountered anyone who could evoke such widely differing opinions

He falls. I move to help him and freeze in my tracks. What am I doing? My officers would have my head if I help him. I would lose everything that I have worked for over the years if I help this man.

He struggles to his feet and we begin again. I start to think about how differently my life might have turned out if I had stood up to my parents.

There are two roads that we face in life: one is living to please others which leads us away from ourselves; the other is a journey of self-love and inner knowledge. I find it strange that suddenly today I am faced with all these insights! The old desires are rushing back to me after all these years of gathering inner dust. Why today? Why are these thoughts beginning again with one simple look from this man with his cross?

He falls again. I walk over to him. He looks at me and, inexplicably, tears well up in my eyes. Imagine me crying at a time like this! I begin to extend my hand to help him up and then, realizing what I am doing, I grab a man from the crowd to carry his cross instead. Thank the gods that at the final moment I came to my senses! I almost helped him! I almost touched him! What is wrong with me? I wish this execution was over with!

To my great relief, we finally arrive at the place of crucifixion. I take the crossbeam from the man who helped carry it and order the one to be crucified to lay down on his cross. I grab his hand and ready the nail. But when my flesh touches his, a strange warmth jolts my body. I look at him and he looks within me. I freeze and, for one brief moment, my mind again reaches back to when I was the happiest. I blink and see him still looking at me. I find the years of inner discipline melting as if they were snow in the sun.

Suddenly there is a loud thump as his flesh is pierced with the metal. Blood spurts as he is one with the cross. He doesn't scream. He doesn't curse. He doesn't even move as the job is finished with two more thumps of the hammer. What kind of man is he? Why is he affecting me so much? Why, after all of these years, am I having second thoughts about my life? As his cross is lifted, and, with a deadening thud, falls into place, my life seems to be falling out of place.

As I take a step backward to take a good look at this man, I find myself moving back in my life. To many, mine was a very successful life. Pulling service in a foreign country is considered an honor. I requested to go to this country knowing that serving under Pilate would be the best way to get ahead. You can get ahead by not listening to the voice inside you, but at the same time never become anything in life. It is far easier to listen to others' opinions about what direction your life should take than to make your own decision. It is a remnant of childhood sometimes too comfortable to give up. To finally strike out on your own is a definite risk. Is it one worth taking? I wouldn't know, for I have given in to listening to the advice of others.

Hanging there between two criminals, the man speaks for the first time. The only word that I can make out is "paradise." Yes, it would be paradise to finally stand up for myself and live what I know is best for me. Paradise...Does such a place exist?

I have been a guard most of my life, but now I realize what I have guarded best is my feelings. In bending to the whims of others, I have lost my sense of self. I would never have chosen to be a guard. But I did choose my destiny when I guarded my own thoughts, my own desires, and what I truly know about myself. I find myself very alone, knowing that there is no one on this earth who truly knows who I am.

He speaks again and once again I only catch a bit of what he is saying... "Forgive them." Forgive them? I find myself thinking of the anger growing within me for all of those people who told me what to do from the time the gift of thought started to grow within me. But my anger serves no purpose other than to cloud the past and fog the future. It was I who handed over my gift of thought to them. They couldn't take it without my acquiescence. There is nothing to be angry with them for. The one that I really have to forgive is myself for following advice I knew was not right for me. It is risky business thinking for yourself. You have no one else to blame if you fail. I have spent many years blaming others for my present state, when in actuality I am the one to blame.

I can feel resolve building within me. I will start again. Who says that we only have one chance at life? Why do we think that when we make a choice it becomes as firm as marble? Why can't we shake the dust of the past and walk freely in our own futures? But I wonder what I would do and where I would go. I shake those thoughts, knowing it would be worse to stay here and be miserable than to walk away into the unknown. Fear can dry out all dreams and make the desert look very appealing.

"I thirst," he says in a very small voice. So do I. So do I.

How is this man on the cross stirring up all my unacknowledged yearning? He is going to die! His life was over as soon as the first nail pierced his flesh! My life may be over too. I, too, felt pierced when his eyes sought my soul and made me rethink what I am doing with the only thing I can truly call my own...my self.

I've earned so many honors and medals, all symbols of doing the bidding of others. Power, prestige, seniority, good placement, moving ahead, moving up, all of these past goals are quickly being reduced to mere trinkets. What is power if you live someone else's aspirations? What is prestige if you put someone else's dreams on your shoulders? What does it mean if you go far but barely take a step on your own inner journey? I have chosen to remain a child rather than grabbing for life and risking everything to be free.

He speaks again: "My mother" is all that I hear. I remember so well the comfort of sitting on my mother's knees and feeling an entire world of possibilities surround me as her arms made my world safe. She was a haven of security who made me feel that I could conquer the world. It is too bad that I outgrew her embrace. My world became someone else's when I climbed down from her lap. I grew into adulthood, when, in reality, I remained a child to anyone who exercised power over me.

He screams now, this King of the Jews. He screams something about God forsaking him. There is no anger but there is pain and confusion all about him. I, too, feel as if I have been forsaken in this life.

I start to turn away from him in my bewilderment. What am I doing? This man can have no answers for me! Just look how he ended up!

I give him one last glance and am struck by his purposefulness. It shines from within his agony. His eyes speak of an inner awareness which I am seeking. He makes his cross his throne.

He bows his head slightly and our eyes lock. He knows me. He knows who I could be. He nods again as if he is giving me permission to be who I always wanted to be. I drop my sword and leave it on the ground, not caring who notices. Let them think what they want!

I move closer to speak to him. Maybe he can help clear up this confusion that is suddenly consuming me. As I take one step closer, I hear him say, "It is finished." He speaks and then he dies. It is finished, for him and for me.

As soon as he dies, I feel a surge of conviction that pushes me to leave my present life and start to live one I choose for myself. Where I will go and what I will do is not important. What is important is that I now have the courage to live my life for me. His life has ended, but my life has just begun. I will say what I think and do what I feel my heart is telling me to do.

I stoop to pick up my sword and stop. I no longer need it. I will leave the sword on the ground along with the rest of my past. I will have no need of it

The other guards are looking at him and at me. I stand very erect before them and speak for the first time with my new voice, not worrying about what they will think. My mind is free for the first time in many, many years as, regardless of the consequences, I boldly proclaim, "This man was innocent beyond doubt. Truly he was the Son of God."

Today is a day I will never forget.

Mary, the Mother of Jesus

When Jesus saw his mother and the disciple whom he loved standing beside her, he said to his mother, "Woman, here is your son."

John 19:26

Mary, the Mother of Jesus

The one major enemy any mother has is time. It robs us of the babes we cradle and rock. Time moves so quickly when it is marked in the growth of our children. A mother's clock is guided by the peaks and the valleys of her children's lives. Days stretch endlessly when she feels her children's pain. Days flee like seconds in the contentment and laughter of her offspring. All too soon, they are grown and a mother becomes painfully aware that time has moved very swiftly.

Standing at the cross of my child, I wish now that I could turn back time. Could I have changed this ending? Could I have warned him about the evil power that I had felt stalking his footsteps? Could I have spoken up for him more than I did even though it was not a woman's place to speak? Relying on the trust I have always had in the ways of the Almighty, I am trying to be strong, for I, like any mother, would prefer to bear his pain instead of the torture of seeing him in such agony.

In a mother's memory, time can be recalled and relived in a heartbeat. I remember I carried him in my womb and smiled as his small feet touched my insides before they touched the ground. The small kicks from my child softened the verbal blows of those who snickered at my pregnancy. These same feet now twist and strain, their freedom restricted by huge nails.

And time stood still for one brief moment as the stars heralded his birth. I felt the universe smiling as this new-born child entered the world in a simple stall reserved for animals. As I held him close to my breast, I fed the one who would feed thousands. All was so very good, and time seemed suspended for just that one moment.

The days passed so quickly—too quickly, I think, as I now would do anything to give my son more time. How easily we forget to cherish the small details until we are faced with the very real possibility of no more time. I wish now that I had control of time and could reverse what I know is about to happen. Parents always expect to outlive their children. I now know that my destiny is to see my only child die at a quickly approaching, predestined time.

Seconds pass so slowly and with every movement of his broken body, my heart is crushed with pain. I feel united with him in agony and suffering. I am his mother. I gave him birth. I brought him into this world. I gave him my milk and my love. I watched him grow. I now must watch him die. If I could only turn back time...

Flashes of times gone by surge through my mind's eye. I vividly recall Cana when he told me it wasn't his time. No mother stands for a child saying they "can't" do something. I think of that day as a "mother's miracle" of determination and affirmation. I pride myself in knowing that I prodded my son into doing something good.

But the time moved so swiftly and suddenly he was leaving me to venture into the world. There was no need for me to be with him as he fed and preached, taught and healed. Like every other mother, I knew the specialness of my child. I had watched him grow and knew that, as much as he belonged to me, he also belonged to a different world. I knew from the heavenly messenger who he was. I knew from the first moment that he stirred inside of me that he was the Promised One. Still, in spite of all my trust and all my faith, I would do anything to turn back time. I want to change this ending and go back to his entry into the city when people threw palms to cover his path. How I wish that I could cover his path now!

He used his short time for the betterment of others. He called people from their slumber of complacency into a complete existence of service and discipleship. He gave them his time, only to be left hanging alone on a cross. True love never deserts anyone in their moment of need. A mother's love never turns its back on her children, even if the whole world has done so.

He fed many with bread and with words. He raised the dead—physically, emotionally, and spiritually. He healed inner scars and outer wounds. Those who forgot how to smile, he taught how to laugh. He healed more than the ten lepers. He sought out the leprosy in each of us and gave us new flesh and new life. His time was spent in sharing timeless moments with those whom time had forgotten. Now he is brought to this time.

I saw him die so many times on his life-giving journey. Only a mother can know the true sorrow and frustration of a rejected prophet. All too often, people took from my son and gave little in return. As he served the needs of others, I was the one to constantly feel his pain, his rejection and his humiliation.

When he was cast from our hometown, I had a terrible foreboding of more rejection to come. Because my own neighbors and the women that I went to market with shuttered the windows of their hearts to my son, the Promised One had to travel to distant places to find those who wanted to have their lives filled.

I remember an old nightmare and know my worst fear is being realized. I hear my child crying and I cannot move to comfort him. So many nights, I, who can sleep even through storms, heard him turn in his sleep and wake up. I was often there before my baby cried in his hunger. I sensed what he needed before he expressed his needs. The memory of nights when he was frightened and called out for me came streaming back to me. It is so ironic that we think of such simple times when things are the most dismal. Now, as I see my son die, all I can offer him is my breaking heart.

I hear him call out my name from his cross. He, like a child again, is asking, "Where is my mother?" I speak words that only he can hear. I scream from my heart, "I am here, my son. Your mother is here. All will be well. Feel my presence. Mother is here."

In a moment that makes me know he is going to die, he gives me as mother to the youngest of his followers, a boy named John. John has a poet's eye and an artist's way of expressing himself. This powerful act of caring for me is so like my son. Even in dying he is concerned for me. So strong is the bond of love between mother and child that nothing on this earth can break its grip.

I hold my breath as he breathes his last. He is dead. My son is dead. My child is gone. My baby is dead. I cry out in agony and beat at the hard wood of the cruel instrument of his death. I never thought that he, who shaped wood with his hands as a boy and shaped lives with his love as a man, would die on the wood of a cross.

As they take his body from the cross, I want to cry out, "Be gentle with my child!" But my child is dead. I cradle his head against my breast and try to give him life once again. As his life-less body rests against mine, another memory, a belief stirs in my heart. I remember his words: "I am the Resurrection and the Life." I know that Jesus, my child, who quieted storms and raised the dead, will not stay dead long.

Never question a mother's intuition. A mother's insights can know more than the most learned scholars. Take this time of rest, my son, and make it be your time. Return to me and let us move together to another time.

I cannot turn back time. But you, my child, son of your Father, control all time. In time I will see you again. In time. In your time, which will always be my time, I will hold you again.

Slowly, I release my baby to be buried in a borrowed tomb.

John the Disciple

In the beginning was the Word, and the Word was with God and the Word was God.

John 1:1

John the Disciple

I feel like an old man and a newborn child at the same time. I feel alone but empowered. I feel frightened but bold, with a whole new sense of purpose. I know he had to die, but it will always be the thing that I least wanted or expected. My very soul screams out in protest, "Not now, not yet..."

I loved him like no other person that ever walked this earth. My love for him was the adoring love that we accord our mothers and the fiercely proud love that we have for our fathers. I grew up in the shadow of his love. He was the large oak tree and I was the acorn that grew beneath his branches. He was the mother bird and I was the baby bird that he fed with love and challenge.

Today the large oak has fallen and the nest is empty, but even in my despair, I am aware of the warmth of the sun's rays, and I am filled with courage to step from the nest and fly. He had to die and leave us before I could change and grow even further.

He always walked in front of me and I gladly followed. He gave and I took. He fed and, daily, I was filled. He taught and I soaked in his words like a dry sponge that knew no saturation. It was a joy to be his disciple. But only through his death could I learn the final lesson—to walk in the lead and to find the dry sponges that exist in everyone. For too long I looked to him to fill every need that my inner being had. Now I can no longer walk with him. Now I must look within to find him. I must walk my own steps and chisel out my own future.

The hardest thing that we face in life is change. But without change we remain baby birds, comfortable in a small nest, never fully expanding our wings, never flying. All too often, we long for change but look to others to change us. In actuality, change is a solitary act of courage that challenges us to feel the wind beneath our wings, only after we leap into flight.

I left the security of home and gladly followed him. I was young and so proud to be accepted in his inner circle. The youngest of the twelve, I was given a favored status. Jesus looked after me just a little bit more than the others, and I reveled in his attention.

I was always amazed at his words and deeds. The more he taught, the more I knew he was a well of inner light. As his message grew greater and bolder, I became more and more convinced that all people would accept and embrace his mission.

He was sentenced to die, not for what he did, but for the personal challenge he gave people to step out of the crowd—to leave behind its security. But they were threatened by his words, so it was easier to kill the messenger than follow the challenge.

Individuals loved him and the crowds despised him. Those who had felt unloved or unaffirmed found themselves changed forever in his company. But people who wanted to keep others confined in the nest knew they had to kill the mother hen and wall in the nest to keep the rest of the birds from flying, from risking change.

He laid out all of the clues to the game of life, but it was not enough for many. They wanted him to move the pieces. So many people desire to change their lives, but when faced with the raw reality of the challenge, they turn their backs on it and resume their normal existence. It is very easy to want to change our lives, and even easier still to do nothing about it, hoping someone else will do it instead. When he did not do this for them, they killed him.

We would love change without pain. We would love to grow but keep our backs turned to the harshest rays of the sun. We would love the nest to be built close to the ground so that our leap would be safer. People want it all but fear the risk. Change takes courage and trust. It takes allowing our feet to follow our hearts. We have to want change so badly that it aches within every fiber of our being and causes us to break through the pain and find our personal antidote.

I am not sure that I know what he wanted for me, but I do know that he allowed me to be me. That is a luxury that few people give to others. That is unconditional love, allowing someone else to stretch their wings and fly. That is power and that is love; that is what made him the Messiah.

He gave me the strength to live my own life and face whatever challenges lie ahead by using the inner tools that he made me realize were mine. He taught me to change by simply being myself. We can spend so much time trying to be like someone else that it can cause us to move further and further from finding who we are called to be. He gave me the courage to be myself

It was very easy to be myself while he stood right next to me or while I walked behind him. Though I now have to face the challenge of walking my own steps and living my own life, I know that I will carry his life within me forever. He taught me to conquer fear by not fearing risks.

His words planted seeds within the garden of my heart. His acceptance of me gave my life new meaning. All that he was for me allowed me to face the challenge of the day when he hung on the cross and we were all crucified together.

As I watched him die, I felt myself moving toward new horizons that I never would have known had he lived. How often I thought to myself that I didn't know what I would do if he ever left me. Now I know the answer was always within me, although I was unaware of it.

He spoke so clearly to everyone that he met. His words held life but he was handed death. He fed so freely, but people became like little demanding birds who wanted to do nothing but stay in the nest and open their mouths. When these big babies chirped their loudest, he moved on to another town. Few realized that food was to be found everywhere if they left the nest.

They killed the messenger of change by misshaping his words and ignoring his good deeds. His enemies saw an easy victim in his gentleness and knew those whom he had touched would have trouble standing up to their evil tactics. During his false trial no one mentioned the good that he left behind.

He spoke so often of his death, but we in the nest did not want to hear any of it. Peter, the bold one, even challenged him to alter his course and avoid his time of change. Poor Peter received a tongue-lashing for speaking what the rest of us were also thinking. No one, not even his friends, wanted to let him be who he knew he must. We did it out of love. Others acted out of fear that he would release the captives that they had imprisoned.

He often spoke in cryptic words. When he told us that a grain of wheat had to die before it would be given new life, I never imagined that he would live out those words himself.

That day he rode the donkey into the city, people were proclaiming him king. The officials demanded that they be silenced. He told them that the very rocks would sing forth his praises. They do so now as they cradle his head in the dark tomb of the man from Arimathea.

He was mother and father to me, brother and friend. He was teacher and mentor, guide and messiah to me. All he asked in return was for me to love him and keep growing, to live free of the shackles that others were ever so quick to put around my hands and my feet, my heart and my mind.

I lived those glorious days at his side. I experienced his healings, his miracles, and his nurturing words. And he loved me. He never gave me a mission as he did Peter. He never looked at me in pain as he did Judas. He never lectured me as he did the two brothers. He never came to visit me as he did Martha, Mary and Lazarus. At the end of each day he would pat the ground and call me close to him. And I grew in his love.

He engendered intense emotions—hatred and love. There was no one who loved him more than I did, and never did I love him more than when we shared that last Passover meal. As he broke the bread, my heart burst with color and my vision cleared. All of his life began to make so much sense. Little did I realize it was nearly at its end.

I laid my head on his chest and listened to his heart. I heard in its beating the hearts of all humanity. Hearing my own heart beating within his brought me the peaceful realization that he was a part of me and I of him. I wanted to keep my head on his chest forever.

The whirlwind of events that followed made my head spin. This man, who did so much good for so many, was dragged through every abuse possible. He held his head up and bore it all with the demeanor of a conquering hero. What he endured I would wish on no one. But he bore our pain with a grace and a purpose that made him part of all who ever lived or would live.

He was mocked. He was disgraced. He was lied about. He was taunted. He was tortured. He was abused both verbally and physically. His message was misconstrued, yet his personhood never wavered. As I stood by his cross with others who saw only his death and destruction, I saw victory about to be born.

As the tears streamed down my cheeks, my heart cried out in anguish. How I longed to lay my head on his chest one last time! I couldn't even touch him, yet I knew my heart was forever entwined with his.

He spoke in tortured phrases during his final, agonizing yet kingly moments. He forgave his persecutors. (Or was he forgiving those who would never have the courage to change their lives?) He screamed out his inner thirst. (Or was it the dryness of those who would never leave the nest?) He called upon our God and allowed people to see that doubting in itself is not bad but a springboard into self-knowledge.

Before he died he gave his mother and me to each other. He knew that I would need to rest my head for a while longer, so I could now rest my head on the bosom of the one who brought him into this world. I will care for this woman who nurtured his life within her. I will watch over her and be step-brother to the one who was everything to me. When her hand touched mine, I once again felt the beating of his heart. Together we felt a new life forming and growing as his spirit left his body

I have no idea where my life will lead me. What I will do does not concern me. Who I will continue to become is the only challenge of my changing life.

His words fill the echoing caverns inside me. His ending was my beginning. My beginning will reflect his words. In the beginning was his word and I must give it flesh. In the beginning was the word and the word became flesh....Maybe I'll write...

Now there was a garden
in the place where
he was crucified,
and in the garden
there was a new tomb,
in which no one had
ever been laid.

And so, because it was
the Jewish day of Preparation,
and the tomb was nearby,
they laid Jesus there.

Early on the first day
of the week,
while it was still dark,
Mary Magdalene came to the tomb
and saw...

John 19:41—20:1